Last Minute Term Papers

By
Ron Fry

THE CAREER PRESS, INC.
Franklin Lakes, NJ

LAST MINUTE TERM PAPERS
Edited and Typeset by Nicole DeFelice
Printed in the U.S.A. by Book-mart Press

To order this title, please call toll-free 1-800-CAREER-1 (NJ and Canada: 201-848-0310) to order using VISA or MasterCard, or for further information on books from Career Press.

**CAREER
PRESS**

The Career Press, Inc., 3 Tice Road, PO Box 687,
Franklin Lakes, NJ 07417
www.careerpress.com

Library of Congress Cataloging-in-Publication Data

Fry, Ronald W.
Last minute term papers / by Ron Fry.
      p. cm.
Includes index.
ISBN 1-56414-605-7 (paper)
1. Report writing—Handbooks, manuals, etc. I. Title.

LB1047.3 .F7963 2002
    808'.02—dc21

           2002067231

Contents

You're not Dead yet... and Neither Is Your Grade

"Time moves slowly, but passes quickly."
—Alice Walker

If you are reading this book, it's probably a safe bet that you did *not* carefully schedule the various steps necessary to write a good term paper. My guess is that many of you suffer from the same feelings of malaise and procrastination that infected my dorm when papers were due. Everyone always seemed hell-bent on finding something, *anything*, that needed to be done...right then. Anything, that is, short of thinking about, researching, outlining, or writing the paper that was due...oh my God, *tomorrow!*

Well, you're saved. Here's a foolproof plan to knock off a paper, no matter how little time you have left:

Write a Great Paper in 24 Simple Steps

1. Sit in a straight, comfortable chair in a clean, well-lighted place with plenty of freshly sharpened pencils.
2. Carefully read over the assignment. Underline or highlight key instructions.
3. Walk down to the vending machines and buy some coffee or a snack so you can concentrate.

4. On the way back to your room, stop and visit a friend from class. If he hasn't started *his* paper, order a pizza. It will help both of you concentrate. If, however, he proudly displays his paper—typed, double-spaced, full of four-color illustrations and bound in one of those irritating see-through plastic folders—hurt him.

5. When you get back to your room, sit in a straight, comfortable chair in a clean, well-lighted place with plenty of freshly sharpened pencils.

6. Read over the assignment again to make absolutely certain you understand it. Highlight key points in a different color.

7. You know, you haven't written to that kid you met at camp since fourth grade—better write that letter now and get it out of the way so you can *really* concentrate.

8. Inspect your teeth in the bathroom mirror. Floss. Twice.

9. Listen to one half of your favorite CD. And that's it, I mean it. As soon as it's over, start that paper.

10. Listen to the other half.

11. Rearrange *all* your CDs into alphabetical order.

12. Phone your friend to see if *he*'s started writing yet. Exchange derogatory remarks about your teacher, the course, the university, and the world at large.

13. Are you sitting in a straight, comfortable chair in a clean, well-lighted place with plenty of freshly sharpened pencils? Great. You deserve a break. Rent "Gone With the Wind" and/or "The Godfather." Parts I, II, *and* III.

14. Read over the assignment again; roll the words across your tongue; savor their special flavor. Choose at least three more highlighter colors.

15. Check the newspaper listings to make sure you aren't missing something truly worthwhile on TV. NOTE: When you have a paper due in less than twelve hours, anything on TV—from "Masterpiece Theater" to "Rocky & Bullwinkle"—*is* truly worthwhile, with only two exceptions: a) Any show involving curling and b) any infomercial featuring Cher.

16. Look at your tongue in the bathroom mirror.

17. Sit down and do some serious thinking about your plans for the future.

18. Open your door; check to see if there are any mysterious, trench-coated strangers lurking in the hall. Thoroughly investigate every corner of the rest of the dorm, just to be safe.

19. Sit in a straight, comfortable chair in a clean, well-lighted place with plenty of freshly sharpened pencils.

20. Read over the assignment one more time, just for the heck of it.

21. Move your chair to a window and watch the sunrise.

22. Lie face down on the floor. Moan and thrash about.

23. Repeat steps 1-22 nightly until there are only 24 hours left before your 25-page paper is due.

24. Leap up and write that paper as fast as you can type!

I received a slightly different version of this exaggerated but all-too-familiar "paper-writing plan" via e-mail from a colleague's fraternity. I hope you enjoyed it. But if you believe this really *is* the way to write a paper, boy, we *are* in trouble!

You know who you are

C'mon, 'fess up—you blew it. You've known about that paper for 12 weeks and haven't done a thing about it. Oh, you *thought* about it often enough—on the way to that ski weekend at the beginning of the semester...before that party last month...when you passed the library last week...as you glanced at the textbook last night. Now you have less than a month, or less than a week, or, heaven forbid, a single day and night left. What the heck are you going to do?

Like cracking the books for the first time the night before a major test and trying to cram a semester's worth of knowledge into your cranium, trying to write an A+ paper (or even a C+ paper) at the last minute usually doesn't work. Nevertheless, we have all burned the midnight oil cramming, writing, or studying... and may well have to do so again.

This book's for you.

This book is written for every one of you—whether it's your fault, or the dog's, or your little brother's—who simply *must* produce at least a *passable* paper in as little as one night. The ideas it outlines are pertinent whether you're a middle school, high school, or college student, an adult going back to school, or an instructor eager to help his or her students salvage something from their procrastination. It is *not* for grades below middle school (which probably don't have to deal with *any* kind of papers yet), nor for those putting off that three-page book report or 10-minute oral presentation. We're talking serious 10-, 15-, even 25-page papers for high school and college-level courses.

After showing you how to do it *right*—the steps to follow and when to follow them, presuming your deadline is from a month to three months away—I'll show you what to do if you've got weeks, days and, yes, *just a single day and night*. And even while showing you the best way to structure, organize, research, write, edit, and proofread your paper, I'll be dropping "Last Minute Tips" along the way.

This book emphasizes those areas where time can be radically "shaved," primarily in the research, writing, and editing stages. So I have moved most of the information about two important steps to Appendices—documenting your sources (formats for creating footnotes, endnotes, and parenthetical notes) and creating your bibliography (including explanations and detailed formats for "Working," "Works Consulted," and "Works Cited" bibliographies).

Thank you Mr. Gates & Mr. Jobs

This book, along with many others on writing and studying that I've written, is ultimately an outgrowth of my best-selling **How to Study**, which is now in its fifth edition. In 1988, when it was first published, I composed it, formatted it, and printed it on (gasp) a personal computer. Barely a decade and a half ago, believe it or else, most people did not *have* a computer, let alone a neighborhood network and DSL, or surf the Web (whatever that was), or chat online, or Instant Message their friends, or...you get the point.

More than anything else, the rapid development of personal computers, software, and the Internet has made the concept of a "last-minute paper" a possibility. If you still had to retype every draft and correct every mistake with that white fluid, the amount of time you would have to allocate just to complete that process would make the term "last minute" almost an oxymoron. (Or significantly limit the number of drafts you could conceivably do in a single day and night to one, perhaps two, putting a premium on your ability to write coherently the first time through.)

As a result, you will find that all of my books, and certainly this one, assume you have a computer and know how to use it—for note-taking, reading, outlining, writing papers, researching, and much more. There are many tasks that may be harder or less efficient on a computer—and I'll point them out—but don't believe for a second that a computer won't help you research and write a better paper in a shorter amount of time, whatever your age, grades, or deadline. (Of course, computers can make your life absolutely miserable, too. As someone once said, "To err is human, to really screw up requires a computer.")

As for the Internet, it has absolutely revolutionized research. Whether you're writing a paper, putting together a reading list, studying for the SAT, or just trying to organize your life, it has become a more valuable tool than the greatest library in the world. Heck, it *is* the greatest library in the world...and more. So if you are not Internet savvy (yes, I'm talking to the parents out there, couldn't you tell?), admit you're a dummy, get a book (over the Internet, of course), and get wired. You'll be missing far too much—and be studying far harder—without it.

Shes, hes, its, and thems

Last but not least, I believe in gender equality, in writing as well as in life. Unfortunately, I find constructions such as "he and she," "s/he," "womyn," and other such stretches to be sometimes (OK, often) painfully awkward. I have therefore attempted to impartially sprinkle pronouns of both genders throughout the text.

Last Minute

Tip: The *less* time you have, the *more* important it is to have access to and experience with a computer, applicable software, and the Net.

Chapter 1

Getting Started the *Right* Way

"Reading maketh a full man, conference a ready man,
and writing an exact man."
—Francis Bacon

Let's just acknowledge here and now that you waited long enough for your paper to qualify as "last minute." You could have as much as a month left to produce an original paper of 50 or more pages, one that *should* take you a semester, if not the whole school year. So presume that these first six chapters are those you can only apply in full the *next* time you have a paper due…and decide *not* to procrastinate. Nevertheless, no matter how little time you have, there are some basics you must still follow. In fact, there are five of them.

Five fundamental rules

Emblazon them on your forehead, if necessary:

Always follow your teacher's directions to the letter.

Always hand in your paper on time.

Always hand in a clean and clear copy of your paper.

Always keep at least one copy of every paper you write.

Never allow a single spelling or grammatical error in any paper you write.

You wanted it typewritten?

Your teacher's or professor's directions may include:

- Choose a specific topic within an assigned general subject area—"some aspect of Teddy Roosevelt's presidency," "a 19th-century novel," "a short story by Gogol, Turgenev, or Tolstoy," "a celestial body outside the Solar System."
- Specific requirements regarding format—typed, double-spaced, include title page, follow APA style, and so forth.
- Suggested length—for example, 10 to 15 typewritten, double-spaced pages.
- Other requirements—turn in general outline before topic is approved; get verbal okay on topic before proceeding; don't include quotes from other works longer than a single paragraph; and/or other idiosyncrasies specific to your own teachers.

Last Minute Tip: Don't screw up a last minute paper that could actually get you a passing grade by failing to follow your teacher's instructions.

Whatever his directions, *follow them to the letter.* Some high school teachers may forgive you your trespasses, but I have known college professors who simply refused to accept a paper that was not prepared as they instructed—and gave the poor but wiser student an F for it (without even *reading* it).

At some point, you'll undoubtedly run into a teacher or professor who is as helpful as a wetsuit in the desert. You ask, "How long?" She says, "As long as it takes." You ask, "Is there any general area within which I should develop a topic?" She says, "Amaze me!"

Use your common sense. If you're in middle school or high school, I doubt she is seeking a 50-page novella. Likewise, if you're in college, it will be difficult to find a professor who thinks a three-page paper is "as long as it takes" or that a book report on *Winnie the Pooh and the Blustery Day* is "amazing."

If you are unsure of a specific requirement or if the suggested area of topics is unclear, it is *your* responsibility to talk to your teacher and clarify whatever is confusing you.

It is not a bad idea to choose two or three topics you'd like to write about and seek preliminary approval from your teacher, especially if the assignment is particularly vague. This will ensure that you do not expend a lot of time and energy on a paper topic the teacher deems "unacceptable"...*after* you've turned it in.

Excuses? We don't accept no stinking excuses!

There is certainly no reason or excuse, short of catastrophic illness or life-threatening emergency, for you to *ever* be late with an assignment, even if you had to stay up all night to do it. Some teachers will simply refuse to accept a paper that is late and give you an F for your efforts. At best, they will accept it but mark you down, perhaps turning an A paper into a B...or worse.

Last Minute Tip: If you are running out of time, ask for an extension! You might get it and have more than enough time to finish your paper (the right way) for the best grade. Warning: The higher your grade in the course, the less likely you'll get a positive response. ("I expect so much more from you...")

What kind of jelly *is* that?

Teachers have to read a lot of papers and shouldn't be faulted for being human if, after hundreds of pages, they come upon your wrinkled, coffee-stained, pencil-written tome and get a bit discouraged. Nor should you be surprised if you get a lower grade than the content might merit *just because the presentation was so poor.*

I am not advocating that you emphasize form over substance—the content is what the teacher is looking for, and he will (should) base most of your grade on *what* you write. But presentation *is* important, teachers are only human (really!), and you can't fault them for trying to teach you to take pride in your work. So follow these simple rules:

- Never handwrite your paper.
- If you're using a computer, put a new ribbon in your dot matrix printer or check the toner cartridge of your laser printer. If you type (or have someone else type) your paper, use clean white bond and (preferably) a new carbon ribbon so that the images are crisp and clear.
- Unless otherwise instructed, always double-space your paper. Leave adequate margins (one inch is normal) all around.
- Use a simple typeface that is clear and easy to read; avoid those that are too big—stretching a five-page paper to 10—or too small and hard to read.
- Never use a fancy italic, modern, or any other ornate typeface for the entire paper.

Last Minute Tip: The *less* time you have to produce a paper, the *more* time you should spend at the end ensuring the best presentation. If you lack the substance, you might as well overhwelm them with form!

Recycling isn't just for cans

There should be a number of helpful messages in your returned papers, which is why it's so important to retain them. What did your teacher have to say? Are her comments applicable to the paper you're writing now—poor grammar, lack of organization, lack of research, bad transitions between paragraphs, misspellings? The more such comments—and, one would expect, the lower the grade—the more extensive the "map" your teacher has given you for your *next* paper, showing you right where to "locate" your A+.

If you got a low grade but there weren't any comments, ask the teacher why you got such a poor grade. You may get the comments you need to make the next paper better. This also shows the teacher you actually care, which could help your grade the next time around.

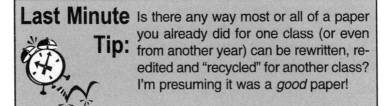

Last Minute Tip: Is there any way most or all of a paper you already did for one class (or even from another year) can be rewritten, re-edited and "recycled" for another class? I'm presuming it was a *good* paper!

Pleeze spel gud

Many employers merrily use resumes and cover letters with grammatical and/or spelling errors for "garbage can hoops" practice. Don't expect your teachers to be any more forgiving—there are definitely a few out there who will award an F without even noticing that the rest of the paper is great. It really *was* too bad you misspelled "Constantinople" or left a participle twisting slowly in the wind.

You *may* sit in a comfortable chair

Here are the *real* steps that, with personal variations along the way, are common to virtually any written report or paper:

1. Research potential topics.
2. Finalize topic.
3. Carry out initial library research.
4. Create temporary thesis and temporary outline.
5. Do detailed library research.
6. Prepare detailed outline (from note cards).
7. Write first draft.
8. Do additional research (if necessary).
9. Write additional drafts.
10. Spell-check and proofread your "final" draft.
11. Have someone *else* proofread.
12. Produce a final draft, including required notes and bibliography.
13. Proofread one last time. Then again.
14. Turn it in and collect your A+.

How long should it take you to write a paper? How much time should you spend proportionately on each step?

Answering the former question depends on the complexity of the topic, the time you have to work with, the relative difficulty of finding appropriate sources, the number of pages, and a host of other factors. The easiest thing to do is simply schedule the above steps so that you utilize the full amount of time until the deadline. One month from the date of assignment? You've got a month to produce your paper. An entire semester? You've got 12 or 14 weeks.

In general, plan to spend a significant amount of the total time available on research, the rest on writing, editing, and proofing. What? Isn't that bass-ackwards? Not at all. Just as Edison famously characterized invention as "99 percent perspiration and 1percent inspiration," I firmly believe that the absolute key to a brilliant (and A+) paper is how you research, structure, and organize your paper. Many professors wouldn't recognize brilliant writing if they fell over it. (Have you ever read some of the papers *they* write?) Still others might admire your style and wordplay but deem them unimportant (your math, science, or even history teachers) and only grade you on *what* you wrote, not *how* you wrote it.

Having said all that, let me give you one suggestion of how to apportion your time, then translate that into days for a few different deadlines:

Steps	By which time you:	Proportion of time
1,2	Finalize your topic	10%
3-6	Complete majority of research	40%
7,8	Complete additional research and first draft	15%
9	Complete all writing	20%
10-14	Turn in your paper	15%

Now, please don't take this as gospel. If you are producing a paper that requires less research but a lot of thought, in which how you write *will* be given greater weight (perhaps one for an English teacher or literature course), these proportions may be totally out of whack. With such an all-encompassing caveat aside, here's how much time I'd allocate to each step using three different deadline scenarios and the above rough proportions:

If you have 12 weeks

Finalize topic, produce temporary thesis and outline	7 days
Detailed library research	35 days
Prepare detailed outline (from note cards)	4 days
Write first draft	4 days
Do additional research (if necessary)	7 days
Write additional drafts; document sources	12 days
Spell-check and proofread "final" draft	3 days

Have someone *else* proofread	3 days
Produce a final draft (with bibliography)	1 day
Proofread final draft and turn in	1 day
Extra time available	7 days

If you have 8 weeks

Finalize topic, produce temporary thesis and outline	4 days
Detailed library research	21 days
Prepare detailed outline (from note cards)	5 days
Write first draft	4 days
Do additional research (if necessary)	3 days
Write additional drafts; document sources	7 days
Spell-check and proofread your "final" draft	1 day
Have someone *else* proofread	1 day
Produce a final draft (with bibliography)	1 day
Proofread final draft one last time	1 day
Turn it in and collect your A+	1 day
Extra time available	7 days

If you have 4 weeks

Finalize topic, produce temporary thesis and outline	2 days
Detailed library research	10 days
Prepare detailed outline (from note cards)	2 days
Write first draft	2 days
Do additional research (if necessary)	1 day
Write additional drafts; document sources	5 days
Spell-check and proofread your "final" draft	1/2 day
Have someone *else* proofread	1/2 day
Produce a final draft (with bibliography)	1/2 day

Proofread one last time and turn it in	1/2 day
Extra time available	4 days

Please use these three suggested plans as guidelines. The first covers roughly a college semester, the second a high school quarter, the third a 4-week course. Each scenario uses a seven-day workweek, so the schedule for 12 weeks, for example, adds up to 84 days. This doesn't mean you have to work seven days a week, just complete that step within a total of seven days (even if you only worked four or five).

Again, I can't tell you *exactly* how much time to set aside for each step, because I don't know any of the specifics about your paper. I *can* tell you that you should plan on consulting and/or taking notes from at least five different sources if you're in middle school (ten if you're in high school, even more in college), whether they be books, articles, Web sites, or other reference materials. Your teacher or subject may demand *more;* I doubt you'll need fewer. And plan on writing two or three drafts of your paper before you arrive at the final copy.

Last Minute Tip: Always allow some "wiggle room" in your schedule—extra days to survive the inevitable times your well-wrought schedule blows up in your face.

Why is attempting to concentrate on some such schedule important? The more time you have to complete a project, the easier it is to procrastinate. If you find yourself leaving such long-term projects to the last week, schedule the projects furthest away—such as the term paper due in three months—*first*. Then, trick yourself—schedule the completion date at least seven days prior to the actual due date, giving yourself a one-week cushion for life's inevitable surprises. We left just such a cushion in each of the above plans. (Just try to forget you've used this trick. Otherwise, you'll be like the perennial latecomer who sets his watch 15 minutes fast in an effort to finally get somewhere on time. Except that he always reminds himself to add 15 minutes to the time on his wrist!)

If you only had the time...

I'm going to spend very little time here talking about time management, which is what "planning" is really all about. (If you are constantly out of sync, I wrote a book called *Get Organized* [Career Press, 1999] that will help you.)

When you know you have to start a paper, especially a last-minute one, be prepared. Stock up on pencils, printer ribbons, computer disks, and any other supplies you need. Otherwise, you may end up running to the store at midnight in search of an elusive printer ribbon or toner cartridge.

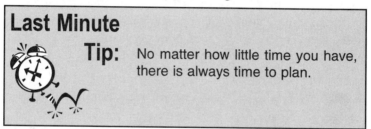

Last Minute

Tip: No matter how little time you have, there is always time to plan.

One great way to maximize your time is to keep (or have immediate access to) a current reading assignment, your calendar, notes for a project, or all three with you *at all times*. You'll be amazed at the amount of work you can get done waiting in line, between classes, or any time you have a few minutes to spare.

And *stay* organized. Keep all materials related to your paper in a separate notebook or file. No messy piles of work scattered here and there, just waiting to be lost or thrown away by mistake.

If you are resolved never to allow "last-minute" to come before another paper, there are some more tips in Chapter 9.

Chapter 2

Choose Your Topic Well

"It isn't working that's so hard, it's getting ready to work."
—Andy Rooney

An A+ paper really starts with a little brainstorming about possible topics. It may start even earlier, when you decide whether to write a *research* paper or a *thesis* paper. The former is much more prevalent in middle school and high school: "Wilma Rudolph: Running For Her Dream," "The Origins of the Common Market," "Wounded Knee and its Legacy," "Stephen Jobs and the First PC." In general, as the name implies, these are papers substantially if not entirely driven by research. (I've seen this referred to as a term paper, a summary paper, and other ways.)

What I call a *thesis* paper is one that actually takes a position that must be proven, that asks a question or that requires real thought, not just "rote" research: "Why drugs should be legalized," "Should drugs be legalized?", "Why the Nagasaki bomb was unnecessary," "How Bush stole the election," "Did Bush steal the election?" (Others have called this an evaluation paper; some even call *this* a research paper. Don't worry about what each is called. Select one or the other based on your own strengths.)

While the latter may sometimes require just as much research, it is a different kind of paper, seeking evaluation rather than just a pure statement of facts. In such a paper, you are asked to interpret these facts (or, at the very least, show how others have interpreted them). And while the former certainly requires "thought," I think you'll find a thesis paper requires a different approach, a different kind of structure and, to some extent, a different way of writing.

Last Minute Tip: By definition, the research paper puts a premium on research and organization. If you know your way around the library and the Internet, take great notes and write logical outlines, select a research paper when given the choice. It will be much easier (*faster*) for you to produce such a paper.

Presuming you know which way you want to go—or your teacher has made the choice simple by *telling* you which way to go—it's time to think of some specific topics. And I didn't say just *one*. Don't settle for just *one* idea—no matter how great you think it is. Be prepared to come up with *several* different possibilities.

In fact, put this book down and go make a list of three or four potential topics right now.

What? You're stuck already? Here are a couple of books to check out in your library. They'll certainly give you a few ideas to mull over:

> *10,000 Ideas for Term Papers, Projects, Reports and Speeches: Intriguing, Original Research Topics for Every Student's Need, 5th Edition*, by Kathryn Lamm (Arco, 1998)
>
> *1001 Ideas for English Papers: Term Papers, Projects, Reports and Speeches*, by Walter James Miller (Hungry Minds, Inc., 1994).

While older (and, I suspect, already integrated into Lamm's book), here are some other potential idea sources:

1000 Ideas for Term Papers in American History, by Robert Allen Farmer (Arco, 1969)

1000 Ideas for Term Papers in Philosophy and Religion, by Brother Uttal (Arco, 1973)

1000 Ideas for Term Papers in Social Science, by Robert Allen Farmer (Arco, 1970)

1000 Ideas for Term Papers in World Literature, by Robert Allen Farmer (Arco, 1970)

Last Minute Tip: Try selecting a topic that would allow you to produce papers for two or more classes *out of the same research!* At the very least, you should be able to do a little extra research, and utilize a good portion of the first paper as the basis for the second. What a great way to maximize your research time!

Do some preliminary research

Got your list of sizzling topics? Then get thee to a library—you need to do a little advance research.

Search your library's card catalog, the *Readers' Guide to Periodical Literature*, and other publication indexes, such as the *New York Times Index, Humanities Index,* or *Biography Index*. Read a short background article or encyclopedia entry about each topic. How many books and articles have been written about each topic on your "possibilities" list? Does there seem to be at least enough material for the kind of paper you're writing, preferably *more* than you could ever need?

Alternatively (or, better yet, additionally), spend a little time online. Are there specific Web sites devoted to your topic? Lucky you! Or does a keyword search result in 10,424 matches, none of which has a *thing* to do with your topic?

While you certainly will want to bookmark helpful Web sites (just as you will want to jot down the call letters of key books and note appropriate magazine, journal, and newspaper articles), do *not* spend time taking copious notes from any of these sources. Remember, the word is "preliminary."

By the time you leave the library or go offline, you should have a general understanding of each of your potential subjects. You will also have identified those topics which might be more difficult to research. Eliminate the latter.

With any luck at all, you should be left with at least one topic that looks like a good research subject. If two or more topics passed your preliminary-research test, pick the one that interests you most.

You're going to spend a lot of time learning about your subject. There's no rule that says you can't enjoy it!

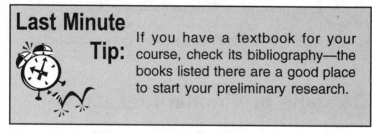

Last Minute Tip: If you have a textbook for your course, check its bibliography—the books listed there are a good place to start your preliminary research.

Give your choice of topic long and careful thought. Pick the wrong topic, and you can write yourself right into disaster.

I'm not implying that you should pick the simplest topic you can find—simple topics often lead to simply awful papers—but there are definitely pitfalls you must avoid. Let's look at the three most common in more depth.

Don't bite off too much

You need to write a 15-page paper for your history class and decide your topic will be "The Battle of the Bulge." Or a 10-page paper for your Religion class and propose to write on "Japanese Buddhism."

Whoa, Nelly! Think about it: Can you really cover topics that broad in 10 or 15 pages? Not unless you trot out a dozen generalities and call it a day. You could write an entire book on either subject (and people have…many).

Instead, you need to focus on a particular, limited aspect of such a broad subject or attack it from a specific angle. How about "The importance of air superiority during the Battle of the Bulge"? Or "The influence of the Taojin monastery on 16th century Buddhist thought?"

Do enough research to make your topic bite size.

But give yourself more than a nibble

By the same token, you must not make your topic too narrow. Choose a subject that's too limited, and you might run out of things to say on the second page of your paper. "Why I don't like Mondays" might make an interesting one- or two-page essay, but it won't fill 10 or 15 pages... even with *really* wide margins.

You can also get into trouble if you pick a topic that is simply over your (academic) head. Oh, sure, there are enough resources—except that many grad students would have trouble summarizing them...and most of them are in French, German, or Croatian. So make sure the plethora of resources you've identified are those *you* can work with.

Or, at least, something to gnaw on

Pick a topic that's too obscure, and you may find that virtually *nothing* has been written about it. (Your premise may be so bogus no one even thought to ask the question!) In which case, you will have to conduct your own experiments, interview your own research subjects, and come up with your own original data. That is, of course, how scientists forge new pathways into the unknown. But I'm guessing that you have neither the time, desire, nor experience to take a similar start-from-scratch approach.

Take it from someone who's done this more than once—it may be wonderfully creative and a lot of fun to work in such original areas, but it can also be frustrating and stressful. And don't underestimate the reaction of your teacher, who may well wish for something a little easier to grade than some far-reaching new theory she really needs to think about. I got a C on the best paper I think I ever wrote. The grad student grading it came right out and told me since he couldn't "check" my ideas—there was nothing published to support my interpretation—he wouldn't give me a better grade.

Don't bite off more than you can chew, but make sure there's *some*thing to gnaw on! And make sure that there are enough *different* sources of material—different authors, different books, and so on—so you can get a well-rounded view of your subject (and not be forced for lack of other material to find ways to make somebody else's points sound like your own).

One last caveat: If you can, avoid choosing a subject area in which your instructor or professor (this applies primarily to college-level courses) is known to have extensive expertise. In the sciences, this could be her current area of research. In the humanities, it could be a topic on which he has written 42 papers.

The danger, of course, is that while your professor will probably know *some*thing about whatever topic you choose, he may know nearly *every*thing about a few. Choose one of those and you will have put yourself in a difficult situation, especially if you disagree (knowingly or unknowingly) with one of his pet theories or interpretations.

Of course, you can't always follow this advice. If you're taking a course on Hemingway from Carlos Baker, his chosen biographer, or a course on James Joyce by one of the preeminent Joycean scholars (I did both), you will be hard pressed to find an area in which the professor *doesn't* know pretty much everything (or think he does)!

Last Minute Tip: It's not unusual to come up with a wonderful topic for which there's a reasonable amount of material, then realize it is simply not right for this particular assignment. Keep your research on this topic. You never know when you'll need to knock off a paper fast.

Develop a temporary thesis

Once you have chosen the topic for your paper, you must develop a *temporary thesis.*

What's a *thesis*, you ask? The word "thesis" is a relative of "hypothesis"—and means about the same thing: the central argument you will attempt to prove or disprove in your paper. It's the conclusion—based upon your research—you draw about your subject.

A thesis is not the same thing as a *topic.* Your topic is what you study; your thesis is the conclusion you draw from that study.

A *thesis statement* is a brief summary of your thesis, summing up the main point of your paper.

Suppose you decide that the topic of your History of Religion paper will be "Changes in 16th Century Catholicism: Catholic Reformation or Counter Reformation?" At the end of your research, you conclude that a case could be made for both. Your thesis statement, then, might look something like this:

> Catholicism in the 16th century changed significantly in structure, doctrine, and personal meaning. These changes can be seen as both a strong reaction to combat the Protestant threat (Counter Reformation) and a spontaneous reform from within (Catholic Reformation).

In your paper, you would try to show how both aspects of your thesis are true, marshaling arguments to illustrate how both perspectives could explain the changes that historically occurred.

Temporary means just that

Note that word *temporary.* No matter how good it looks to you now, your temporary thesis may *not* wind up being your final thesis. Because you haven't completed all your research yet, you can only come up with a "best-guess" thesis at this point.

You may find out during your research that your temporary thesis is full of holes or simply doesn't hold up. If that's the case, you will revise it, perhaps even settling on a thesis that's the exact opposite of your first! In fact, you may revise your thesis *several* times during the course of your research.

If a temporary thesis doesn't spring easily to mind—and it probably won't—sit back and do some more brainstorming. Ask yourself questions like:

- "What's special or unusual about ____?" (Fill in the blank with your topic.)
- "How is ____ related to events in the past?"
- "What impact has ____ made on society?"
- "What do I want the world to know about ____?"
- "What questions do I have about ____?"

The answers to these and similar questions should lead to several good thesis ideas. If you find yourself needing more information about your topic to answer these questions, do more reading.

Ask your instructor

Some teachers require you to submit your thesis statement for their approval prior to beginning your paper. Even if this is *not* required, getting your instructor's opinion is always a good idea. She will help you determine whether your thesis argument is on target, and, if not, perhaps how to fix it.

Create a temporary outline

Once you have developed your temporary thesis, think about how you might approach the subject in your paper. Jot down the various issues you plan to investigate. Then, come up with a brief, temporary outline of your paper, showing the order in which you might discuss those issues.

Let's presume you uncovered an old magazine article that revealed how a number of civilian women pilots were recruited by the Air Force during World War II to supplement the men in uniform. You decide to write a paper on "The role of women pilots during World War II." Although it's a pretty broad subject, you have to write a 20-page paper and feel this will give you more than enough material to work with. Based on your preliminary research, you create a general, temporary outline of your paper:

- A. Why they entered war effort
- B. Type and number who participated
- C. Qualifications and training
- D. Missions
- E. Contributions
- F. Civilian vs. military argument
- G. Disbanding group
- H. Their fight to be recognized as veterans

Don't worry too much about this outline—it will be brief, at best. It's simply a starting point for your research, a plan of attack. It's certainly possible, for example, that you could wind up focusing on a single aspect of this overall topic—their missions and contributions or their fight for recognition.

And note that you have not included either an introduction or conclusion. These will be added outside the outline, since they will be structured and written only *after* you've completed your research, finalized your thesis statement, and developed your detailed outline. Don't worry: We'll be spending a lot of time on *them*.

Chapter 3

Doing Research and Taking Notes

"Some books are to be tasted, others to be swallowed, and some few to be chewed and digested."
—Francis Bacon

Having done preliminary research, chosen a topic, and developed a temporary thesis and outline, this is the point at which you need to declare your topic choice final. In other words, if you are going to change your topic, now is really the time to do it, before you spend a significant amount of time doing real research and taking notes.

The obvious place to begin your hunt for research materials is the library. Today's libraries offer an amazing variety of resources—learn how to tap into their mother lode of information and you'll be much richer. If you have gotten this far in life *without* being introduced to library basics, just ask a librarian for help. (As a matter of fact, even if you consider yourself something of a library expert, always ask your librarian for help!) Tell her what you're working on—she'll invariably know the best sources of information and where to find them.

You may find so many potential resources that you won't have time to read them all. Concentrate on those that have been published most recently or written by the most respected sources. However, don't limit yourself *too* much—gather information from a wide range of sources. Otherwise, you may learn only one side of the story.

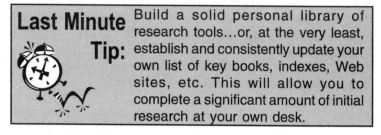

Last Minute Tip: Build a solid personal library of research tools...or, at the very least, establish and consistently update your own list of key books, indexes, Web sites, etc. This will allow you to complete a significant amount of initial research at your own desk.

Most libraries are divided into reading rooms, restricted collections, and unrestricted book stacks. Unrestricted book stacks are those through which anyone using the library can wander, choosing books to use while in the library or, if allowed, to take home. Restricted areas generally include any special collections of rare books, those open only to scholars or those with particular credentials, either by library rule or by order of whoever donated the collection (and, often, the room housing it) to the library. In some libraries, *all* book stacks are closed, and *all* books must be obtained from a librarian.

Most libraries contain both *circulating materials*—those books and other items you may check out and take home with you—and *noncirculating materials*—those that must be used only in the library. All fiction, general nonfiction, and even most "scholarly" titles will usually be found in the first group. Reference material, periodicals, and books in special collections are usually in the second.

At most libraries, many of those old, familiar library tools—like the trusty card catalog—have been replaced by computerized systems. These can be a little intimidating for first-time users, but they are great time-savers. Again, don't be shy about asking for help. Your librarian will be happy to show you how to operate the computers.

How your library is organized

"A man's library is a sort of harem."
—Ralph Waldo Emerson

To provide organization and facilitate access, most small and academic libraries utilize the Dewey decimal classification system, which uses numbers from 000 to 999 to classify all material by subject matter. It begins by organizing all books into 10 major groupings:

000 - 099	General
100 - 199	Philosophy
200 - 299	Religion
300 - 399	Social Sciences
400 - 499	Language
500 - 599	Natural Science and Mathematics
600 - 699	Technology
700 - 799	Fine Arts
800 - 899	Literature
900 - 999	General Geography and History

Given the millions of books available in major libraries, just dividing them into these 10 groups would still make it quite difficult to find a specific title. So each of the 10 major groupings is further divided into 10 and each of these now one hundred groups is assigned to more specific subjects within each large group. For example, within the philosophy classification (100), 150 is psychology and 170 is ethics. Within the history classification (900), 910 is travel and 930 is ancient history.

There is even further subdivision. Mathematics is given its own number in the 500 series—510. But specific subjects within mathematics are further classified: 511 is arithmetic, 512 is algebra, and so on.

Finally, to simplify your task even more, the last two digits in the Dewey code signify the type of book:

01 Philosophy of
02 Outlines of
03 Dictionary of
04 Essays about
05 Periodicals on
06 Society transactions and proceedings
07 Study or teaching of
08 Collections
09 History of

If your library doesn't use the Dewey system, it probably is organized according to the Library of Congress system, which uses letters instead of numbers to denote major categories:

A: General works (encyclopedias and other reference)
B: Philosophy, Psychology, and Religion
C: History: Auxiliary sciences (archeology, genealogy, etc.)
D: History: General, non-American
E: American history (general)
F: American history (local)
G: Geography/Anthropology
H: Social sciences (sociology, business, economics)
J: Political sciences
K: Law
L: Education
M: Music
N: Fine arts (art and architecture)
P: Language/Literature
Q: Sciences
R: Medicine

S: Agriculture
T: Technology
U: Military science
V: Naval science
Z: Bibliography/Library science

Just be aware that the two classification systems bear *no* relation to each other. You can't just say, "Oh, that geometry book's Dewey number is 513.024. If I just add 5, multiply by 2 and subtract the day of the week, I'll have it's Library of Congress call letters." No. Sorry.

There's an encyclopedia about *that?*

In your elementary school days, you probably relied on one of the tried and true encyclopedias—World Book, Britannica, Grolier's, Collier's—when you had to write a report. While such broad reference works are still a reasonable starting point (though you'll probably be consulting them online), there are a surprising number of topic-specific encyclopedias, dictionaries, and almanacs available in many libraries. While a college-level paper may well require significant additional research, many middle school and even high school students will find an abundance of research material in just one of these resources.

In a single monthly issue of *Library Journal*, the trade magazine for librarians, I recently found reviews of the following just-published titles: *Encyclopedia of Rainforests, Encyclopedia of African History and Culture, Encyclopedia of World Music, Dictionary of American Literary Characters, Encyclopedia of Crime and Justice, Encyclopedia of Nursing and Allied Health, Medieval Folklore, Rivers of the World, The Encyclopedia of Christmas, Dictionary of Theology, Encyclopedia of Deserts, Encyclopedia of Smoking and Tobacco, Oxford Companion to Food* and (my favorite) the *Charlie Chan Film Encyclopedia*.

Needless to say, there was an equally impressive list of newly available CD-ROMs and new reference Web sites.

This broad array of general resources should make it increasingly easy to choose a good topic, establish a reasonable thesis, and gather enough information to construct an initial outline, without having to do any further research.

But unless you are *still* in elementary school, completing an A+ paper will require you to turn to other sources for more detailed information. You need to read books written by experts in the field you're researching, as well as magazine and newspaper articles about every aspect of your subject.

Why stop there? Pamphlets, anthologies, brochures, government documents, films, and videos are just some other possible sources of information for your paper.

Just remember: Never use a single resource as the basis for all or even most of your paper, no matter how short the paper, no matter how pertinent the book. Why?

- Most, if not all, teachers frown on a single book bibliography. Many will specify a minimum number of bibliographic listings (usually not less than 10 at the high school level, more in college and above).
- Who says the author's right or even accurate? Do you want your grade based on someone whose credibility is somewhere between zero and nada?
- It's far too easy to inadvertently plagiarize.

Where to look for materials

How do you find out whether anyone has written a magazine or newspaper article about your topic? How do you know if there are any government documents or pamphlets that might be of help? How do you locate those written-by-the-experts reference books?

You look in your library's publication indexes, which list all of the articles, books, and other materials that have been published and/or are available in your library. Most are arranged alphabetically by subject.

Some of the major publication and online indexes are listed below. There are others—ask your librarian for suggestions.

1. **The card catalog.** This is a list of all the books in your library. (Although many libraries now store it on computer, it's still often called a card catalog because it used to be kept on index cards.) Books are indexed in three different ways: by subject, by author, and by title.

2. **Book catalogs**, the best-known of which are *Books in Print*, *Forthcoming Books* and the *Cumulative Book Index*.

3. **Newspaper indexes.** Several large-city newspapers provide an indexed list of all articles they have published. Your library may even have past issues of one or more available on microfiche.

4. **Periodical indexes.** To find out if any magazine articles have been published on your subject, go to a periodical index. *The Readers' Guide to Periodical Literature,* which indexes articles published in the most popular American magazines, maybe one with which you're familiar.

5. **Vertical file.** Here's where you'll find pamphlets and brochures.

6. **Guide to U.S. Government Publications, American Statistical Index,** and **Congressional Information Service Index.** These are all useful for locating government publications.

Using online resources

If you're under the age of 30 (or maybe even 40), I certainly don't have to spend a lot of time touting or explaining the research value of the Internet.

Even just a few years ago, it was not really possible to do extensive research just using the Web or Internet. Now there's so much material it's easy to be overwhelmed. While it can be extremely helpful to have access to some obscure Web sites that have just the material you need, especially when a book or two you want to take notes from has disappeared from the library, I am still convinced that most of you will waste too much time if the majority of your research is done online. I can attest from far too much personal experience that it is ridiculously easy to get sidetracked when doing research online. "Wow, I didn't know there were that many cool sites about bungee jumping. I'd better check them out...right now!"

Be careful about two things:

1. While much of the "basic" information on most research-oriented Web sites is not going to radically change day to day, that is certainly not true of all sites. Just as the identical keyword search may yield radically different results if run on two separate days (or two different search engines), you may find material you needed deleted the next time you look for it. So if you find something really good, download it, save it to your hard drive, print a hard copy.

2. Anyone can post information on the Web, whether they're qualified or not, whether the material is accurate or not. Make sure your sources are reputable so your teacher doesn't question the validity of your information.

Virtually all of the widely used periodical indexes—covering American and world history, art, biology, philosophy, religion, psychology, engineering, and much more—are available on the Web. And most magazines, newspapers, encyclopedias, government organizations, and so forth have Web sites that can be a starting point for your search. They often have links to other sites where you can find full-length articles and stories, biographical information, and the like.

Online bookstores (amazon.com, bn.com and, if you're Canadian, chapters.indigo.ca) will list many books even before they're published, almost always before your local library has ordered, cataloged and shelved them. Their recent feature of including searchable pages from many titles—from a table of contents and short excerpt to 50 pages or more—should help you get a feel for whether the book or a portion of it is pertinent to your topic. If you have the time, you can then order it, gaining access to a resource you wouldn't be able to consult any other way.

Amazon in particular offers a "People who bought this book also bought" feature, a good way to locate related resources (especially since none of the online bookstores make searches by subject easy or accurate).

An approach to online research

I am indebted to Robin Rowland, author of *The Creative Guide to Research* (Career Press, 2001), for the following suggestions on how to maximize your ability to research online:

- Long before a paper is due, choose four search engines—one a meta-search engine (which searches other search engines), the other three regular. Robin's recommendations: Copopernic (meta), Google, Hotbot, AltaVista, Northern Light, Dogpile (meta).
- When beginning your research, use the meta engine first.
- Learn each engine's advanced features—you'll find things faster and easier.
- Print out the FAQ pages for each search engine and create your own manual.
- Choose three search engines with different strengths to maximize your search abilities.
- Consider using a specialized search engine, such as Beaucoup, if you are unable to find what you want or have found too much information.
- Learn Boolean searches.
- If you require very specialized data—summaries of legal cases, relatively obscure technical and

academic journals, certain government data—it
may not be on the Web or Internet. If necessary,
consider accessing a proprietary database such as
Dialog, Lexis-Nexis or Dow Jones. Careful—they
can be expensive. Check with your librarian to see
which are available and whether a fee is charged.

Your working bibliography

To create your working bibliography (that's right, the
books you're "working with"), you'll need a supply of 3 x 5 (or
4 x 6) index cards. You can buy these for next to nothing at
most dime stores, bookstores, and office stores. (You'll also
use index cards when you take notes for your paper, so buy a
big batch now. A few hundred cards ought to suffice.)

While you're stocking up on index cards, pick up one of
those little boxes designed to hold the cards. Put your name,
address and phone number on the box. If you lose it, some
kind stranger may return it. If not, after you duplicate all of
your work, I guarantee you'll never lose one again.

Step 1: Create your bibliography cards

You'll complete the first step of the bibliography three-
step at the library. Take your index cards, a couple of pens or
pencils—and this book, of course.

Start a systematic search for any materials that might have
information related to your paper. Look through the indexes
we discussed earlier and any others your librarian recommends.

When you find a book, article, or other resource that looks
promising, take out a blank note card. On the front of the
card, write down the following information:

> **In the upper right-hand corner of the card:** Write
> the library call number (Dewey decimal number
> or Library of Congress number), if there is one.
> Add any other detail that will help you locate the
> material on the library shelves (Science Reading

Room, Reference Room, Microfiche Periodicals Room).

On the main part of the card: Write the author's name, if given—last name first, followed by first name, then middle name or initial. Then the title of the article, if applicable, in quotation marks. Then the name of the book, magazine, newspaper, or other publication—underlined.

Add any details you will need if you have to find the book or article again, such as:

- Date of publication.
- Edition—"third (1990) edition" for a book; "morning edition" for a newspaper.
- Volume and/or issue number.
- Page numbers on which the article or information appears.

In the upper left-hand corner of the card: Number it. The first card you write will be #1, the second, #2, and so on. If you happen to mess up and skip a number somewhere along the line, don't worry. It's only important that you assign a different number to each card.

At the bottom of the card: If you're going to do research in more than one library, write the name of the library. Also write down the name of the index in which you found the resource, in case you need to refer to it again.

Do this for *each* potential source of information you find, *and put only one resource on each card.*

Some experts in the research-paper business have different ideas about what goes where on bibliography cards. It's not really important—if you prefer to put the elements of your card in some different order, it's okay.

Just be sure that you're consistent so you'll know what's what later on. And leave some room on the card—you'll be adding more information when you actually get the reference material in your hands.

Step 2: Prepare your working bibliography

Copy the information from each of your bibliography cards onto a single list. As you do this, follow the bibliography style rules outlined in Appendix B. (These rules cover bibliographic minutiae—where to put periods, how many spaces to indent lines, and so forth.) When you have finished your list—your working bibliography—make a photocopy or two. Keep one copy with your research file, another in a safe place in your room or desk.

The final bibliography, a required part of your paper, lists resources from which you gathered information. Your *working* bibliography contains all the resources from which you *might* gather information.

Step 3: Start taking notes

You may be used to keeping your notes in a three-ring binder or on a notepad. I'm going to show you a note-taking system I think is better—you'll record all of your notes on your blank index cards.

As was the case with your bibliography cards, you must follow some specific guidelines to make this method work. You'll want to refer to the guidelines in this chapter often during your first few note-taking sessions. After that, the system will become second nature to you.

Once your first bibliography card is finished, set it aside. Get out some blank index cards and start taking notes from your first reference source. Follow these guidelines:

- Write one thought, idea, quote, or fact on each card. If you encounter a very long quote or string of data, you can write on both the front and back of a card, if necessary. *But never carry over a note to a second card.*
- What if you *can't* fit the piece of information on one card? You're dealing with too much

information at once. Break it into two or more smaller pieces, then put each on a separate card.

- Write in your own words. Summarize key points about a paragraph or section, or restate the material in your own words. Avoid copying things word for word.

- Put quotation marks around any material copied verbatim. It's okay to include in your paper a sentence or paragraph written by someone else to emphasize a particular point (providing you do so on a limited basis). But you must copy such statements *exactly as written* in the original—every word, every comma, every period. You also must *always* put such direct quotes within quotation marks in your paper and credit the author.

- It's essential that you paraphrase what the author has written *when you actually take the note*. This will protect you from unintended plagiarism. (Just ask historians Doris Kearns Goodwin or Stephen Ambrose about what fun *that* is.) You will not want to waste time going back to check every source. And don't think just changing a word or two protects you. You really have to absorb what the author said and then put it in your own words.

As you finish each note card, do the following:

- In the upper left-hand corner of the card, write down the resource number of the corresponding bibliography card (from its left-hand corner). This will remind you where you got the information. It is *not* necessary to also number each card (1-1, 1-2, 1-3, etc.) unless you have some inexplicable desire to see how many note cards you've used.

- Below the resource number, write the page number(s) on which the information appeared.

- Get out your preliminary outline. Under which outline topic heading does the information on your card seem to fit? Under your "A" heading? Under "C"? Jot the appropriate main topic letter in the upper right-hand corner of your note card. Do *not* use any but the broadest divisions of your preliminary outline (A, B, C, etc.), as you may well make extensive changes to your outline as you go along.

If you're not sure where the information fits in your outline, put an asterisk (*) instead of a topic letter. Later, when you do a more detailed outline, you can try to fit these "miscellaneous" note cards into specific areas.

- Next to (or below) the topic letter, jot down a one- or two-word "headline" that describes the information on the card (which will help you place it within the general topic).
- When you have finished taking notes from a particular resource, put a check mark on the bibliography card. This will let you know that you're done with that resource, at least for now.

Sample Completed Note Card

2	B
p. 55	unemployment/compliance

Two-thirds all working-age disabled people still unemployed–same portion jobless when law passed.

Be sure that you transfer information accurately to your note cards.

Double-check names, dates, and other statistics.

As with your bibliography cards, it's *not* vital that you put each of these elements in the exact places I've outlined above. You just need to be consistent: Always put the page number in the same place, in the same manner. Ditto with the resource number, the topic heading, and the headline.

Add your personal notes

Throughout your note-taking process, you may want to create some "personal" note cards—your own thoughts, ideas, or impressions about your subject or your thesis.

Perhaps you've thought of a great introduction for your paper. Put it on a card. Or maybe you've thought of a personal experience that relates to your topic. Put it on a card.

Write each thought on a separate note card, just as you have with information you've taken from other resources. Assign your note card a topic heading and mini-headline, too. In the space where you would normally put the number of the resource, put your own initials or some other symbol. (I use "M" for "Mine.")

Keep an eye out for new resources

When you look up information in one reference book, you'll often find leads to additional resources. Check to see if these resources are on your working bibliography. If not, and you think they are worth consulting, add them. Make up a bibliography card for each new source, too.

Throw away unprofitable leads

If a particular resource doesn't yield any useful information, take the bibliography card for that resource out of your stack. Stick it away in your card file, just in case you want it later.

Or, if you're certain that you won't want to refer back to the resource, throw the bibliography card away altogether.

Then scratch the listing from your working bibliography. Don't waste precious time renumbering your remaining cards—it doesn't matter if a number is missing. (However, *keep every card if you must supply a "Works Consulted" Bibliography.*)

As you go through your sources, keep asking yourself questions:

- Is what the author saying so pertinent and perfectly worded that I want/need to quote directly? The answer to this question will have an effect on how quickly you're able to fill out that particularly card. If you decide to paraphrase, you can resort to some of the shorthand tips I discuss a little later. Just be careful to use quotation marks if you *have* copied directly, so you won't think you've already paraphrased.

- Does this material support/contradict the facts/opinions of another author?

- Which one do I believe? If there is contradictory evidence, what should I do? Should I refute it? *Can* I refute it? If it supports my position, does quoting it add anything to my paper?

- Where does this material fit? Some material won't fit neatly into the preliminary outline you developed. Which is why it's important to place one and only one thought on a card. You may even change your outline as a result.

How to streamline your note-taking

There are some simple ways to save a lot of time when you're taking notes, whether for a paper or in class:

- Eliminate vowels and articles: "? shld FDR hve dn?" is a lot faster to write than "What should Franklin Roosevelt have done?"
- Use word beginnings: "Rep" for "representative," "reptile" or "Republican"; "sym" for "symbol,"

"symbiosis," or "symmetry"; "adv" for "advantage," "adversary," or "advertisement." It's especially helpful to abbreviate words or even phrases that are going to appear frequently in your notes.

● Never use a period after an abbreviation: They add up!

● Use standard symbols in place of words. Here's a short list you can use whenever and wherever you have to take notes. You'll probably recognize many of them from your math, logic, or science classes:

$\approx$	Approximately
w/	With
w/o	Without
wh/	Which (or what)
$\rightarrow$	As a result of
+	And, also
*	Most importantly
cf	Compared to
ff	Following
<	Less than
>	More than
=	Same as, equals
$\uparrow$	Increasing
$\downarrow$	Decreasing
Esp	Especially
Δ	Change
$\therefore$	Therefore
$\because$	Because

Create your own symbols and abbreviations. As long as you are comfortable with your own shorthand, feel free to substitute other symbols for frequently used words or concepts. Just be careful if you start using the same or similar abbreviations in separate classes to mean two entirely different things. And don't use an abbreviation ("K" for the "Kinetic Theory of Gases") that is already a generally accepted abbreviation in the same subject ("K" for "degrees Kelvin").

What some of the pros use

There are some heavy-duty, free-form databases, such as askSam, Info Select and Scholar's Aid, that are probably more familiar to your professors than to you (and certainly to me). I suspect they are far more than most of you would ever need to organize your notes, unless, perhaps, you are working on a major project, such as a thesis. Robin Rowland's *The Creative Guide to Research* (Career Press, 2000) discusses these in great detail.

Before you are done

The shorter your deadline, the less easily you can return to the library or even go online to fill in major gaps in your paper. So as you're taking notes, keep "writing the paper in your head," adding each note in its proper place. While it is usually quite normal to have to set aside some time for additional research, the *less* time you have, the *more* likely you won't be able to.

So consider quickly sorting through your cards by general category while you're still at the library. Do you have the facts, statistics, ideas, arguments and examples you think you need? Are there any obvious "holes"? It's better to identify—and fulfill—areas of need while you're still in "research mode" than to have to schedule another trip to the library.

Chapter 4

Organizing Your Paper

"Order and simplification are the first steps toward the mastery of a subject."
—Thomas Mann

"If a man can group his ideas, he's a good writer."
—Robert Louis Stevenson

Your research is done.

Which means—if you proportioned your time as I suggested earlier—that at least *one-half* of your *paper*, perhaps as much as *three-quarters* of it, is done, even though you've yet to write one word of the first draft. (And you'll soon find you have done a great deal of *that* already, too!)

You've finished going through all of those reference materials listed in your working bibliography. You've completed your bibliography cards. You've uncovered a lot of information about your subject. And you've taken extensive notes. It's time to organize your data.

You need to decide if your temporary thesis is still on target, determine how you will organize your paper, and (perhaps) create a detailed outline.

Review, then finalize your thesis statement

Take a close look at your temporary thesis statement. Does it still make sense, given all the information your research has uncovered? If it doesn't, revise it now.

Your research should have led you to *some* conclusion about your subject. This, in turn, should lead you to the final thesis of your paper.

Structure your paper

Once you have your final thesis, begin thinking about how you will organize your paper. Virtually any term paper you write will use one of these nine ordering sequences:

1. **Chronological:** Discusses events in the order in which they happened (by time of occurrence).

2. **Spatial:** Presents information in geographical or physical order (from north to south, top to bottom, left to right, inside to outside, and so forth).

3. **Numerical/Alphabetical:** An obvious way to organize a paper on "The Ten Commandments" or "The Three Men I Admire Most," for example.

4. **Major division:** For topics that logically divide into obvious parts.

5. **How to:** How to grow an orchid, write a better paper, etc. Like this book, organizes material from "what to do first" to "what to do last."

6. **Problem/solution (cause/effect):** Presents a series of problems and possible solutions, why something happened, or predicts what *might* happen as a result of a particular cause.

7. **Effect/cause:** Discusses a condition, problem or effect and works *backward* to what might have caused it.

8. **Compare/contrast:** Discusses similarities and differences between people, things, or events. May also be used when you want to discuss advantages and disadvantages of a method, experiment, treatment, approach, etc.

9. **Order of importance:** Discusses the most important aspects of an issue first and continues through to the least important, or vice versa. (A slight variation of this is organizing your paper from the **known** to the **unknown**.)

10. **Pro/con:** Arguments for and against a position, question, decision, approach, method, etc.

The first four sequences are considered "natural," in that the organization is virtually demanded by the subject. "A Day in the Life of..." would probably begin at dawn and end at midnight. A paper on "The physical destruction of 9/11" that was organized spatially could begin at Ground Zero and continue, in ever-increasing geographical circles, to describe the damage. A lab report, which would include sections on materials and equipment, procedures, results and conclusions, is a good example of a paper organized by major division.

The other sequences are "logical," in that the order is chosen and imposed by *you*, the writer. If you're writing about an environmental issue, you might utilize the problem/solution sequence: Looser environmental laws resulted in more air pollution which led to greater incidences of respiratory diseases which led to higher death rates among children and seniors... The effect/cause sequence starts with the effect and then examines the causes: Higher death rates among the young and old in a particular area are a result of a concentration of manufacturers releasing large quantities of pollutants into the water supply.

If you were doing a paper on the development of new training techniques for elite runners, you could start by discussing the *most* effective new technique(s) and end with the least effective (organizing your paper by *decreasing importance*) or start with the least effective and work your way to the most revolutionary (*increasing importance*).

The *general-to-specific* starts with a wide-ranging statement (the "big picture") and adds more and more detail to explain it, amplify it, or justify it. *The specific-to-general* begins with facts (specifics) and uses them to reach a larger conclusion.

Finally, a *pro-con* organization is useful when you intend to present both sides of a controversial idea or subject without necessarily supporting one or the other ("The arguments for and against the legalization of drugs").

Note that in many cases the actual order you choose is also reversible—You can move forward or backward in time, consider cause and effect or effect and cause, etc. So you actually have a dozen and a half potential ways to organize your material!

Your subject and thesis may determine which organizational approach will work best. If you have a choice of more than one, use the one with which you're most comfortable or that you feel will be easiest for you to write. (Nobody says you *have* to choose the hardest way!) Keep in mind that you can use a *blend* of two approaches—for example, you might mention events in chronological order and then discuss the cause/effect of each.

For now, stick with the structure you selected when you wrote out your temporary outline. Take all of your note cards and sort them:

- Group together all of the cards that share the same outline topic letter—in the upper right-hand corner of each card—A, B, C, etc.
- Put those different groups in order, according to your temporary outline, A on top of B on top of C, etc.
- Within each topic group, sort the cards further. Put together all of the cards that share the same "headline"—the two-word title in the upper-right hand corner.

- Go through your miscellaneous topic cards—
those marked with an asterisk. Can you fit any of
them into your existing topic groups? If so, replace the asterisk with the topic letter. If not,
put the card at the very bottom of your stack.

Decide on the order of your paper

Your note cards now should be organized according to
your temporary outline. Take a few minutes to read through
them, beginning at the front of the stack and moving right
through to the end. *What you are reading is a rough sketch of
your paper*—the information you collected in the order you
(temporarily) plan to present it. If you did a good job taking
and organizing your notes, you should be lacking an introduction, conclusion, some transitional phrases and, perhaps, a
fact or example or two. That's all (hopefully).

Look at your preliminary outline. Is it organized the way
that makes the most sense now that you've completed your
research? Take a little time to go through your note cards.
Read each one. Think about what you have already written.
Does another structure come to mind? For example, perhaps
you had planned to use chronological order—to tell readers
what happened, in the order that it happened. After review-
ing your note cards, you decide that it would be better to take
a cause/effect approach—to discuss, one by one, a series of
different events and explain the impact of each.

Rearrange your cards

If necessary, revise your still-general outline according to
the organizational decision you just made. However, *don't*
change the letters that you have assigned to the topics in your
outline. If you decide to put topic "B" first in your new outline, for example, keep using the letter "B" in front of it. Otherwise, the topic letters on your note cards won't match those
on your outline.

If you revised your outline, reorder your note cards so that they fall in the same order as your new outline. Then go through each group of cards that share the same topic letter. Rearrange them so that they, too, follow the organizational pattern you chose.

After you sort all of the cards that have been assigned a specific topic heading, review the cards that are still marked with an asterisk or your initials. Try to place them in your stack of cards.

Don't force a note card in where it doesn't belong. If there just doesn't seem to be *any* logical place for the information on the card, it may be that the data *isn't* relevant to your thesis. Set the card aside in a "leftover" pile. You can try again later.

And while you're setting aside inappropriate notes, don't forget to seek out "holes" in your paper—those areas that cry out for a more up-to-date fact, a good example, a stronger transition. No one likes to discover the need to do a little more research, but if *you*'ve identified the omission, I guarantee that your teacher will notice it. Don't let a "black hole" turn a potentially great paper into one that's merely okay…just because you don't want to spend another hour online or in the library.

Your detailed outline is done!

Flip through your note cards from front to back. See that? You've created a detailed outline without even knowing it. The topic letters on your note cards match the main topics of your outline. And those headlines on your note cards? They're the subtopics for your outline.

Last Minute Tip: If you've done a good job organizing your notes and the paper "flows" when you read through your cards, you *don't* have to create a separate paper outline (unless your teacher requires one). That's a real time-saving aspect of the note-card system.

Some instructors like to approve your outline before letting you proceed with your paper. If yours does, find out the specific outline format you are to follow. You may need to use a different numbering/lettering format from the one shown in this book—Roman numerals instead of capital letters for topic headings, for example.

Otherwise, you can get as detailed as you like with your outline. In most cases, a two-level outline—with topic headings plus subheadings—will suffice. Remember that you must have a minimum of two entries at every level of your outline.

Many word processing programs have automatic outline functions. Becoming familiar with this feature could well save you significant time.

Here's a sample detailed outline for the paper on women pilots in World War II:

A. Why civilian women pilots entered the war.
   1. Shortage of male pilots
   2. Women pilot proposal
   3. Beginnings of test program

B. Who participated
   1. Number of initial participants
   2. Background info on leaders of program
   3. Socio-economic background of participants

C. Qualifications and training
   1. Experience needed for acceptance into program
   2. Training
      a. Ground school
      b. Flight school
      c. Exams

D. Missions and contributions
   1. Ferrying planes
   2. Towing targets
   3. Testing repaired planes
   4. Success vs. male pilots

E. Military vs. civilian status
   1. Why initial civilian status?
   2. Plan to militarize
   3. Why plan needed
   4. Why not carried out

F. Disbanding of group
   1. Additional pilots no longer needed
   2. Male pilots wanted jobs previously taken by women
   3. Arguments for/against disbanding

G. Fight to be recognized as veterans
   1. Importance of
      a. Veterans' benefits for women
      b. Recognition of contributions
   2. Key women in fight
   3. Debate and vote in Congress
   4. Outcome and effect of vote

If you look at your own final outline—or at the cards that produced it—you should be able to clearly spot holes, plus any areas where you still want to rearrange, particular points you want to drop entirely, whatever... *all before you have ostensibly written a single word of your paper.* By focusing this intently on your notes and their organization, you are to some extent making the actual writing almost an afterthought.

Chapter 5

Writing Your First Draft

"I always do the first line well, but I have trouble doing the others."

—Moliere

For some reason, this step is the hardest for most people. It's psychological, I guess—a fear that when your thoughts actually appear in black and white, there for all the world to read, you'll be judged a complete fool.

Well, you can't do a research paper without writing. And since the job has to be done, you might as well face it right now.

You may not have realized it, but you've already *done* a lot of the hard work that goes into the writing stage. You have thought about how your paper will flow, you have organized your notes, and you have prepared a detailed outline. All that's left is to transfer your information and ideas from note cards to paper.

Still, as a writer, I know that this can be a scary prospect, no matter how well you've done up to now. So, in this chapter, I'll show you some tips and tricks that will make writing your rough draft a bit easier.

If possible, "write" directly onto a computer so that you can add, delete, and rearrange your words easily. Don't worry if your computer software doesn't have all the latest bells and whistles—a simple word-processing program is all you really need.

But do keep a hard copy of your latest version. Hard disks do crash. Check out whether your software allows you to track changes and easily save and compare different versions, as Microsoft Word (which I use) does.

It's *supposed* to be rough

If you go into this thinking you're going to turn out a teacher-ready paper on your first try, you're doomed. That kind of performance pressure leads only to anxiety and frustration.

At this point, your goal is to produce a rough draft—with the emphasis on *rough*. Your first draft isn't *supposed* to be perfect. It's *supposed* to need revision.

Relax your expectations, and you'll find that your ideas will flow much more freely. You'll be surprised at the intelligent, creative thoughts that come out of that brain of yours when you're not so worried about making a mistake.

The walls will come later

The essence of good writing has little to do with grammar, spelling, punctuation, and the like. The essence of good writing is good thinking.

Sure, the mechanics of writing are important. Before you turn in your paper, you will need to ensure that you have everything spelled just right, that your participles aren't dangling, your periods and commas are placed just so.

But your thoughts, ideas, and logic are the foundation of your paper, and you need to build a foundation before you worry about plastering the walls. So, for now, just concentrate on getting your thoughts on paper. Don't worry about using exactly the "right" words. Don't worry about putting commas in all the right places. Don't even worry about grammar at all. We'll take care of all that polishing later.

Do a note-card draft

Your note cards helped you come up with a detailed outline. Now, they're going to serve you again—helping you plot out the paragraphs and sentences of your paper.

We're going to do some more sorting and rearranging of cards. The end result will be what I call a "note-card draft." Here's what you do:

1. Your note cards should be arranged in the same order as your detailed outline. Take out all of the note cards labeled with the letter of the first topic on your outline.
2. Out of that stack, take out all the cards marked with the same "headline" as the first subheading in your outline.
3. Look at the information on those cards and think about how the various statistics, quotes, and facts might fit together in a paragraph.
4. Rearrange those cards so they fall in the order you have determined is best for the paragraph.

Here's an example using our "women pilots" paper. Suppose you had 30 cards that fit in the first major topic—"Why civilian women pilots entered the War." Of these, four had information related to the first subtopic—"shortage of male pilots." Here's the information on each card:

Card #1: Quote from a general about the severity of the pilot shortage.

Card #2: Statistics about the number of pilots needed vs. those available for active duty.

Card #3: Explanation from Congressional committee hearing of why there was a shortage.

Card #4: Description of types of jobs not getting done.

How would you make these four disparate bits of information into a winning paragraph? Here's one solution:

1. Start with a statistic showing the need and establishing its severity (card #2).
2. Explain the reasons for the shortage (card #3).
3. Discuss the jobs that needed to be filled as a result of the shortage (card #4).
4. Wrap up with the general's quote, which serves to summarize and emphasize the key point of the section (card #1).

Presuming you agreed with this suggested order, you would just shuffle the note cards accordingly, then move on to the next subtopic. Little by little, paragraph by paragraph, you could map out your entire paper in this way.

Build your paper, brick by brick

Each paragraph in your paper is like a mini-essay. It should have a topic sentence—a statement of the key point or fact you will discuss in the paragraph—followed by the evidence to support it. You shouldn't expect your reader to believe that your topic sentence is true just because *you* say so—you must back up your point with hard data. This evidence can come in different forms, such as:

- Quotes from experts.
- Research statistics.
- Examples from research or from your own experience.
- Detailed descriptions or other background information.

Paragraphs are like bricks of information—stack them up, one by one, until you have built a wall of evidence. Construct each paragraph carefully, and your readers will have no choice but to agree with your final conclusion.

If paragraphs are the bricks in your wall of evidence, transitions—a sentence or phrase that moves the reader from one thought to another—are the mortar that holds them together.

Smooth transitions help readers move effortlessly from the summary of one paragraph to the introduction of another. (The first sentence in the paragraph you have just read is an example of a transition.)

Now put it all on paper

It's time to take the plunge and turn your note-card draft into a written rough draft. Using your cards as your guide, sit down and write.

Double- or triple-space your draft—that will make it easier to edit later. After you are finished with each note card, put a check mark at the bottom.

If you decide that you won't include information from a particular card, don't throw the card away—yet. Keep it in a separate stack. You may decide to fit in that piece of information in another part of your paper or change your mind after you read your rough draft and include the information where you had originally planned.

You may, however, wind up with cards that just don't fit. If you're convinced they have no place in your paper, don't attempt to shoehorn them in anyway. Put them aside. As Johnny Cochran would say, "If they blow the flow, those notes got to go."

When it's just not working...

Got writer's block already? Here are a few tricks to get you unstuck:

- **Bribe yourself.** Establish a pleasant reward you'll give yourself as soon as you reach your preset goal. Make it a good one! If you get sidetracked, feel like procrastinating or start to lose your focus, remind yourself of that great reward that's just around the paragraph, and get back to work!
- **Pretend you're writing to a good friend.** Just tell him or her everything you've learned about your subject and why you believe your thesis is correct.

- **Use everyday language.** Too many people get so hung up on using fancy words and phrases that they forget that their goal is to *communicate*. Long, multi-syllabic words are usually more abstract than shorter, simpler ones. So spending too much time "thesaurusizing" is, ultimately, self-defeating.

- **Just do it.** What is it about a blank computer screen or piece of paper that scares would-be writers so badly? It happens to almost everyone, and there's only one cure I know: Just type something ...*anything*. Once you have written that first pargraph—even if it's a really *bad* first paragraph—your brain will start to generate spontaneous ideas. If not, go ahead and write a really shabby second paragraph, and an absolutely *atrocious* third paragraph. Just keep on writing. Copying your notes, word for word, onto your computer is a solution for the worst writer's block.

- **Don't edit yourself!** As you write your rough draft, don't keep beating yourself up with negative thoughts, such as "This sounds really stupid" or "I'm a terrible writer. Why can't I express that better?" Remember: Your goal is a *rough* draft—it's supposed to stink a bit.

- **Keep moving.** If you get hung up in a particular section, don't sit there stewing over it for hours—or minutes. Just write a quick note about what you plan to cover in that section, then go on to the next section. Force yourself to make it all the way through your paper, with as few stops as possible.

- **Write the concluding paragraph first.** It is, after all, just a "fleshed-out" version of your thesis statement, so it should be pretty easy. And reminding yourself where your paper is *supposed* to be heading may make it easier for you to write the rest of it.

It's supposed to be *your* work

It's so tempting. You're having trouble with a sentence or section. The information you need was explained beautifully in that article you found in an old magazine. Why not just copy that perfectly written section from the article? It's such a musty and obscure journal your teacher couldn't *possibly* be familiar with it. Why not use it?

Because that would be plagiarism—passing off another person's words or ideas as your own—which is probably the only "mortal sin" in writing. It's a sure way to bring your grade down, down, down. It may even "earn" you a failing mark, a suspension or (*shudder*), expulsion. And, those disasters aside, it is simply *wrong*.

"But who'll ever know that I didn't write it myself?" you wonder. Sorry, but the odds are about 999 to 1 that you *will* be found out. Your teachers are smarter than you think.

Remember, your teacher probably has been reading research papers—some of them undoubtedly on the same subject as yours—for a good many years. And those same "perfect passages" tend to pop up again and again. Do you *really* think your teacher will believe it's a coincidence that you wrote the same paragraph, word for word, as that student in *last* year's class? Yes, *that* one. The one who *flunked*.

Also, your teacher is familiar with your work and writing style. That "borrowed" paragraph, written in someone else's style, is going to be noticeably different than your own deathless prose, kind of like a new Mercedes in a parking lot full of used Yugos.

Think the vastness of the Internet will save you? Sorry, there's new software being released almost constantly to help teachers spot info you found on (and freely borrowed from) the Web. I expect, given the recently headlined cases at the University of Virginia and elsewhere, that many more teachers will be using such tools to catch cheaters.

Then, of course, there is the moral issue involved—but I won't get into that. You learned that stealing was wrong in kindergarten. It's a principle that applies to written words and ideas, too.

And don't forget that the shorter the deadline, the more tempting it is to "borrow" that well-crafted paragraph...or page...or paper. Resist the temptation, and you won't lose any sleep waiting for the inevitable other shoe to drop.

A little rewriting music, maestro

To avoid plagiarism, you must give proper credit to the original author of material you use, even if you paraphrase it. You must also give credit for any facts, figures, or research data that you use. You do this through a *source note*—a footnote, endnote, or parenthetical note. See Appendix A for the correct way to format each.

Sometimes, you *will* want to include a sentence or entire paragraph exactly as written by another author. If so, you must enclose the material in quotation marks and copy the material word for word, comma for comma. You must also offset the paragraph from the rest of the paper by indenting it from both margins, like this:

> "The author's paragraph you're quoting word for word is set off from the rest of the section by indenting it from both margins. It also is enclosed in quotation marks."

Use direct quotes sparingly, and only if the segment is so eloquently written or so meaningful that it will make (you hope) a special impact on the reader.

You should *not* do this to fill up your paper the "easy" way—if your teacher is anything like most of mine, he won't welcome seven pages of quotes in a 10-page paper.

Besides, it's not that hard to blend facts into your paper along with the pertinent attribution. You just need to cite the person, who they are (or why anyone should believe them) and where the information came from. Then paraphrase it.

For example: As former General Electric CEO Jack Welch suggested in his book, *Jack: Straight From the Gut,* the best sales representatives do not necessarily make the best sales managers.

Chapter 6

Editing, Rewriting, and Proofreading

"A good style should show no sign of effort. What is
written should seem a happy accident."
—W. Somerset Maugham

One way or another, you managed to get *something* on
paper, even if your first draft would give Stephen King night-
mares. It's time to take that rough-cut diamond and polish it
into a sparkling gem. In this chapter, we'll revise your rough
cut—and revise it again—until we arrive at your final draft.

As we've done with other parts of your assignment, we'll
break this process into several steps.

In this chapter, we'll work through three of those steps.

First, you'll edit your paper for content and clarity.

Then, you'll work on the finer points—grammar, spelling,
sentence construction, and so forth.

Last, you'll proof, proof, and re-proof in an effort to catch
every single spelling, grammatical, and factual error. It's the
one phase during which being a perfectionist is not only good,
it's *mandatory*.

Say what you mean

"Read over your composition, and whenever you meet with a passage which you think is particularly fine, strike it out."

—Samuel Johnson

As I said, we're not going to handle all your revisions in one pass. At this point, you still don't need to concentrate on grammar, spelling, and other technical aspects of your paper. Of course, if you notice flaws in any of these areas as you read through your paper, fix them, just don't go looking for them right now.

Rather, during *this* phase of the revision process, you should be trying to:

- Improve the flow of your paper—from paragraph to paragraph, sentence to sentence, word to word.
- Organize your thoughts and information better.
- Clarify any confusing points.
- Strengthen any weak arguments—by explaining your argument better or adding more data to support your point of view.

As you review your rough draft, ask yourself the following questions:

- Do your thoughts move logically from one point to the next?
- Is the meaning of every sentence and paragraph crystal clear?
- Does every sentence make a point—or support one?
- Do you move smoothly from one paragraph to the next? Or do you jump randomly from one topic to another?

- Do you support your conclusions with solid evidence—research data, examples, statistics?
- Do you include a good *mix* of evidence—quotes from experts, scientific data, personal experiences, historical examples?
- Do you have a solid introduction and conclusion?
- Did you write it in your own words and style? Or have you merely strung together phrases and quotes "borrowed" from other authors?
- Have you explained your subject thoroughly? Or assumed that readers have more knowledge about it than they actually might?
- Have you convinced your readers that your thesis is valid?
- Is there information that, while correct and informative, just doesn't belong? Cut it out!
- Have you maintained a consistent point of view (first, second, or third person throughout)?
- Does your last paragraph successfully summarize the entire paper and effectively "close" your argument?

Mark any trouble spots with a colored pencil or pen. If you have an idea of how to fix a section, jot it down on your rough draft.

Then, ask a friend or parent to read your paper. Ask *them* which sections were confusing, which didn't seem to fit in as written. Make notes on your draft about these trouble points.

Now, sit down and begin to rewrite. Focus on all of those problem areas you found. If necessary, add new information. Play with sentences, paragraphs, even entire sections.

If you're working with a computer, this is fairly easy to do. You can flip words, cut and add sentences, and rearrange whole pages with a few keystrokes.

If you're still hunched over a typewriter or scratching along with pen and paper, you can do the same thing, using scissors and tape. Just cut up the pages of your rough draft and tape them together in their new order.

If you can't figure out how to fix a bothersome sentence or paragraph, take some time out from writing. Think about what it is you're trying to tell the reader—what point are you trying to get across?

Once you get your thoughts straight, the words will usually take care of themselves.

Work on your "headline"

I dare say if you asked your teacher, she would never admit that the first and last paragraphs of your paper are far more important than the rest. "Oh, no," she'd sparkle, "I plan to read every word of your immortal prose and savor each delightful syllable."

Right.

Whether she admits it or you believe it, first and last impressions *do* matter. I urge you to spend a significant amount of time polishing, polishing, *and re-polishing* every word of your opening and closing paragraphs. And, of course, make sure they say exactly what you want them to say.

Your paper's opening paragraph is the most important of all. It sets out what you will be arguing for or against (and why you chose that side) or introduces the rest of the paper. If it's well written, it will seamlessly lead your teacher into the rest of the paper *and* earn you points for solid organization. If it's poorly written, it may not matter what follows—your teacher may conclude you obviously don't know what you're talking about and grade accordingly (*while spending less time than he might have otherwise on the rest of the paper*).

Think of the introduction and the conclusion as the bread in a sandwich, with the information in between as the hamburger, lettuce, tomato, and pickle. The main attraction may be what's between the slices, but you don't even have a sandwich without the bread.

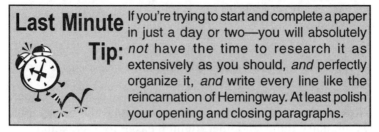

Last Minute Tip: If you're trying to start and complete a paper in just a day or two—you will absolutely *not* have the time to research it as extensively as you should, *and* perfectly organize it, *and* write every line like the reincarnation of Hemingway. At least polish your opening and closing paragraphs.

Here are some ways to start off your paper with a little zing:

- Say something that grabs attention.
- Say something controversial.
- Paint a picture of a scene.
- Recreate an event.
- Use a potent quote.
- Ask a provocative question.

But don't—*do* absolutely *not*—use a joke. The joke will be on you. Most teachers have no sense of humor once they start grading papers (presuming they did before).

Check the facts

When you finish editing for content and meaning, print a clean copy of your paper.

It's time to double-check all of your facts for accuracy.

Comb through your paper and check *every* piece of factual information against your note cards:

- Did you spell names, terms, and places correctly?
- When you quoted dates and statistics, did you get your numbers straight?
- Do you have a source note (or preliminary source note) for every fact, expression, or idea that is not your own?
- If you quoted material from a source, did you quote that source exactly, word for word, comma for comma? Did you put the material in quotation marks?

Mark any corrections on your new draft. Again, use a colored pen or pencil so you'll easily spot corrections later.

Smooth out the edges

You've already fixed major problem areas in your paper. Now take an even closer look at your sentences and paragraphs. Try to make them smoother, tighter, easier to understand.

- Use action verbs and the active voice: "Some apes in captivity have survived for thirty or more years" is better than "Ages of thirty years or more have been enjoyed by some apes in captivity." "She seemed unwilling to accompany him" is weaker (and wordier) than "She refused to accompany him."

- Consider dropping constructions beginning with "there is (was)" from your vocabulary: "There was a storm at sea" is a tired and boring way to proclaim, "A storm raged."

- Is there too much fat? Seize every opportunity to make the same point in fewer words. "Although she was late…" is better than "In spite of the fact that she was late…"

- Are there places where phrasing or construction is awkward? Try to rearrange the sentence or section so that it flows better.

- Did you use descriptive, colorful words? Did you tell your reader, "The planes were damaged" or paint a more colorful and creative picture: "The planes were broken-down hulks of rusted metal— bullet-ridden, neglected warbirds that could barely limp down the runway."

- Consult a thesaurus for synonyms that work better than the words you originally chose. But don't get carried away and use words so obscure that the average reader wouldn't know their meaning.

- **Misspelled words**. Check every word. Ask yourself: "If I had to bet $100 that I spelled that word correctly, would I pull out my wallet?" No? Then you'd better look it up in the dictionary! Watch out for words your spell-check program may not catch, such as "too" instead of "to" or "your" instead of "you're."
- **Incorrect punctuation**. Review the rules regarding placement of commas, quotation marks, periods, and other punctuation. Make sure you follow those rules throughout your paper.

Should you include graphics?

If a picture is worth a thousand words, can you just include four pictures and forget having to write that 15-page paper? No, but nice try. However, there may well be instances when including a chart, graph, diagram, or some such element will both spruce up the look of your paper and help illuminate a concept better than words ever could.

Consider including some form of graphics:

- When describing a complex process, such as how water from a dam creates hydroelectric power.
- When a chart or graph can better encapsulate mathematical data, such as changes in respiration rates, in one-minute intervals, during a marathon.
- When a map would help the reader visualize what you're talking about, such as the changes in downtown New York since 9/11.
- Whenever it would make the paper look more presentable, help you organize your data, and/or help the reader understand your point.

Your inclusion of a graphic element of any kind—chart, graph, diagram, table, drawing, photograph, etc.—should *accentuate* the text, not merely be an attempt to cover up bad

When in doubt, opt for the familiar word rather than the obscure, the shorter vs. the longer, the tangible vs. the hypothetical, the direct word vs. the roundabout phrase.

- Have you overused cliches or slang expressions? Especially in academic writing, neither are particularly appreciated. Your paper may be "dead as a doornail" if you don't "get the lead out," get rid of some of the "oldies but goodies," and make sure your paper is "neat as a pin."
- Have you overused particular words? Constantly using the same words makes your writing boring. Check a thesaurus for other possibilities.
- How do the words *sound?* When you read your paper aloud, does it flow like a rhythmic piece of music? Or plod along like a funeral dirge?
- One of the best ways to give your writing a little "oomph" is to vary your sentence structure. Use short sentences occasionally. Even very short. Without subjects. Use simple sentences, complex sentences (an independent clause and one or more dependent clauses), and embedded sentences (combining two clauses using relative pronouns rather than conjunctions). And despite what Mrs. Dougherty taught you in 8th grade, it really *is* okay to start sentences with "and" or "but". And to use sentence fragments for emphasis and effect. Really.
- Always remember the point of the paper: to communicate your ideas as clearly and concisely as possible. So don't get lost in the details. Yes, we've all heard of one famous writer or another (Flaubert comes immediately to mind) who filled a wastebasket with discarded pages before he got one page of usable prose. Whose every word seemed to be drawn screaming and kicking from

his distended belly. Hey, this isn't *Madame Bovary* you're writing here. Relax. If you have to choose between that "perfect" word and the most organized paper imaginable, opt for the latter.

Again, mark corrections on your draft with a colored pen or pencil. No need to retype your paper or enter your changes yet—unless your draft is getting so marked up it's difficult to decipher!

Now check grammar and spelling

Here's the part that almost nobody enjoys. It's time to deal with those things I've been urging you to delay—correcting sentence structure, grammar, punctuation, spelling, and so on.

I've told you all along that your thoughts are the most important element of your paper. It's true. But it's also true that glaring mistakes in grammar and spelling will lead your teacher to consider you either careless or downright ignorant. Neither of which will bode well for your final grade.

So, get out your dictionary and a reference book on English usage and grammar. If you don't happen to own the latter, check one out of the library or, better yet, buy one. (This won't be the last time you'll use it, so it's a good investment.) Ask your instructor to recommend a few good choices.

Scour your paper, sentence by sentence, marking corrections with your colored pen or pencil. Ferret out:

- **Poor subject-verb agreement**. Use a singular verb with a singular subject, make it plural when the subject is plural: "The ice cream sandwich was delicious" but "The ice cream cones were awesome."

- **Incorrect pronoun-antecedent agreement**. If you replace a noun (the antecedent) with a pronoun, the pronoun must agree with the verb (just as the subject had to): "The superintendent didn't show up, but he rarely does on Sundays.

- **Inconsistent verb tense**: "I was hitting a golf ball and my swing is was wrong."
- **Run-on sentences**: "I wish I knew what went wrong (;) I could have done something else.
- **Dangling modifiers**: "Employed as a weatherman in Indianapolis, hailstones as big as canned hams were predicted by current talk-show host David Letterman." Hint: Identify the subject (hailstones) and ask yourself if the phrase modifying it makes sense. I don't think even Indianapolis employs hailstones as weathermen.
- **Faulty parallelism**: "To be considered great, an NFL running back must be able to change direction, to run with power, a good IQ is helpful, see and hit the "holes," durability is important." Hint: Reread the sentence using just the subject and each phrase, one at a time. Here's the correct way to write it (and test parallelism): "An NFL running back must run with power, (…must) be able to change direction, (…must) be smart, (…must) be able to see and hit holes, and (…must) be durable."
- **Too many simple sentences begging to be combined**: "The two friends were practicing hockey. They were on an ice floe. It was near their village. It was huge. It was flat." Try a simple combination sentence instead: "The two friends practiced hockey on a huge, flat ice floe near their village."
- **Problems with the most confused or misused words**: its/it's; you're/your; weather/whether; their/they're/there; to/two/too; principal/principle; affect/effect; conscience/conscious; accept/except; than/then; who's/whose; among/between; eminent/imminent/immanent; all ready/already; lay/lie; all together/altogether.

writing and/or poor organization. If it's not explained, placed in the proper context, nor supported in the text itself, adding an illustration adds nothing.

Prepare the *almost*-final draft

Now get back on the computer and make all of those corrections you marked as you completed each of the previous steps. (Or retype your paper incorporating all of those corrections.) As you prepare this draft of your paper, incorporate the following three steps:

1. Format the paper according to your teacher's instructions—use the specified page length, margins, and line spacing. If you haven't been given any instructions in this area, follow these guidelines:

   - Type or print on one side of the paper only.
   - Use 8 1/2 x 11 paper.
   - Leave a one-inch margin all around—top, bottom, right, and left.
   - Indent the first word of each paragraph five spaces from the left margin.
   - Double-space all text. (Single-space footnotes, but double space between each.)
   - Number your pages in the upper right-hand corner of the paper, one half-inch from the top.

2. Incorporate your final footnotes, endnotes, or parenthetical notes. For specifics on how to do this, see Appendix A.

3. Give your paper a title, if you haven't already done so. Your title should be as short and sweet as possible, but should tell readers what they can expect to learn from your paper. Don't get cute or coy.

You may want to have a title and a subtitle—for example, "Women Air Force Service Pilots: The Almost-forgotten Veterans of World War II." If so, separate your subtitle from the title with a colon and two spaces.

Some teachers prefer that you put your title, name, date, and class number on a separate title page. Others want this information to appear at the top of the first page of your text. As always, ask your instructor which page format to follow. (And consult the style manuals listed in Appendix B for specific formats.)

Now, give yourself a big pat on the back! The toughest parts of your assignment are all behind you.

Make it perfect

To be a good proofreader, you need a sharp eye. Unfortunately, your poor eyes are probably pretty tired by now. And you've become so familiar with your paper that it may be difficult for you to see it clearly. You're likely to read phrase by phrase, rather than word by word (and certainly not letter by letter). And that means that you'll likely skip right over some typos and other errors.

Another problem is that our brain often convinces us we're seeing what we *expect* to see. I recently published a book that, according to the spine, was titled "The War World II 100." When it was handed to me and I was asked to read it aloud, looking right at it, I "read," "The World War II 100."

In this section, I'll show you some tricks that will help you overcome these problems and catch all those little bugaboos in your manuscript.

Read your paper aloud

Go to a quiet room and read your paper aloud. Not in your head—actually speak the words you have written. Sound them out, syllable by syllable. You'll quickly identify an uncomfortable number of typos and misspelled words.

Circle any errors that you find with a brightly colored pen or pencil. You want to be able to spot them easily and quickly when you type up your final draft.

Work backward

This is another great trick. Read your paper from back to front, starting with the last word on the last page, working backward toward your introduction. This will force you to focus on each individual word, rather than on the meaning of your phrases and sentences.

Use your computer's spell-check

If you're working on a computer that has a spell-check program, be sure to use it. But don't rely on it alone! Yes, the computer will pick up misspelled words. But what if you've used the wrong *word* altogether—used "their" when you meant "there"? If you've *spelled* it right, the computer won't pick up your error (though a grammar/usage program probably will).

Have someone else read your paper

Ask a parent, sibling, or other relative to read your paper. Or trade papers with a classmate—you'll look at his if you can show him yours. Someone who has never seen your paper before is much more likely to catch a mistake than someone who has read it again and again. Just be careful about the person you pick and the instructions you give her. You don't want to hear from your lovely but anal-retentive friend—an hour before your paper is due—how *she* would have organized it.

Prepare your perfect copy

After you've proofread your paper several times *(at least* three times), type or print out a clean draft. Then proofread it *again,* to make sure you caught every single error. Miss one or two? Print those pages again *and proofread again.* Continue until you're sure your paper is error-free. Then proofread it one more time (and I'm willing to bet real money you will still find at least one mistake).

Remember that you are checking three distinct areas: content, spelling and grammar, and format. Don't do a great job on the first two and forget to number your pages or include your bibliography!

Get it all together

Be sure to put your final draft on good quality, white bond. Don't use that erasable typing paper—it smudges easily.

If you've written your paper on a computer, avoid printing your final draft on a low-quality dot matrix or bubble-jet printer. Manuscripts printed on such printers are sometimes hard to read—and the last thing you want to do is make it difficult for your teacher to read your paper. (Some instructors do not even accept such copies.)

Last Minute Tip: If you're writing a paper on a weekend or overnight, your content is unlikely to earn you a top grade. You'd better concentrate on the presentation and hope it conceals some of your paper's basic shortcomings.

You can also save your paper on a floppy disk or Zip disk and take it to a quick-print shop. Providing you're working on a compatible computer system, they can print out your paper on a laser printer, which produces typeset-quality printing. If your school has a computer lab, there might be a few good-quality printers available there as well.

If you don't have access to a good printer, or if you're just a lousy typist, you may want to have your final draft prepared by a professional typist or computer service bureau. Just make sure the one you select can have your paper done in plenty of time to meet your final deadline!

As soon as you complete your final draft, head right for the copy shop. Pay the buck or two it costs to make a copy of your paper. In the event that you lose or damage your original manuscript, you will have a backup copy.

Here's a great tip: Type the file name for your report right at the top of your copy. That way, if you ever have to refer back to the report, you'll know exactly where to find it on your hard drive. This is especially important if you're not using long file names and have to remember what Jdtxthis.doc stands for!

Turn in your assignment

Put your paper in a new manuscript binder or folder, unless your instructor asks you to do otherwise. Then, turn in your paper—on time, of course!

When in doubt, opt for the familiar word rather than the obscure, the shorter vs. the longer, the tangible vs. the hypothetical, the direct word vs. the roundabout phrase.

- Have you overused cliches or slang expressions? Especially in academic writing, neither are particularly appreciated. Your paper may be "dead as a doornail" if you don't "get the lead out," get rid of some of the "oldies but goodies," and make sure your paper is "neat as a pin."

- Have you overused particular words? Constantly using the same words makes your writing boring. Check a thesaurus for other possibilities.

- How do the words *sound?* When you read your paper aloud, does it flow like a rhythmic piece of music? Or plod along like a funeral dirge?

- One of the best ways to give your writing a little "oomph" is to vary your sentence structure. Use short sentences occasionally. Even very short. Without subjects. Use simple sentences, complex sentences (an independent clause and one or more dependent clauses), and embedded sentences (combining two clauses using relative pronouns rather than conjunctions). And despite what Mrs. Dougherty taught you in 8th grade, it really *is* okay to start sentences with "and" or "but". And to use sentence fragments for emphasis and effect. Really.

- Always remember the point of the paper: to communicate your ideas as clearly and concisely as possible. So don't get lost in the details. Yes, we've all heard of one famous writer or another (Flaubert comes immediately to mind) who filled a wastebasket with discarded pages before he got one page of usable prose. Whose every word seemed to be drawn screaming and kicking from his distended belly. Hey, this isn't *Madame Bovary* you're writing here. Relax. If you have to choose between that "perfect" word and the most organized paper imaginable, opt for the latter.

Again, mark corrections on your draft with a colored pen or pencil. No need to retype your paper or enter your changes yet—unless your draft is getting so marked up it's difficult to decipher!

Now check grammar and spelling

Here's the part that almost nobody enjoys. It's time to deal with those things I've been urging you to delay—correcting sentence structure, grammar, punctuation, spelling, and so on.

I've told you all along that your thoughts are the most important element of your paper. It's true. But it's also true that glaring mistakes in grammar and spelling will lead your teacher to consider you either careless or downright ignorant. Neither of which will bode well for your final grade.

So, get out your dictionary and a reference book on English usage and grammar. If you don't happen to own the latter, check one out of the library or, better yet, buy one. (This won't be the last time you'll use it, so it's a good investment.) Ask your instructor to recommend a few good choices.

Scour your paper, sentence by sentence, marking corrections with your colored pen or pencil. Ferret out:

- **Poor subject-verb agreement**. Use a singular verb with a singular subject, make it plural when the subject is plural: "The ice cream sandwich was delicious" but "The ice cream cones were awesome."
- **Incorrect pronoun-antecedent agreement**. If you replace a noun (the antecedent) with a pronoun, the pronoun must agree with the verb (just as the subject had to): "The superintendent didn't show up, but he rarely does on Sundays.

- **Inconsistent verb tense**: "I was hitting a golf ball and my swing ~~is~~ was wrong."
- **Run-on sentences**: "I wish I knew what went wrong (;) I could have done something else.
- **Dangling modifiers**: "Employed as a weatherman in Indianapolis, hailstones as big as canned hams were predicted by current talk-show host David Letterman." Hint: Identify the subject (hailstones) and ask yourself if the phrase modifying it makes sense. I don't think even Indianapolis employs hailstones as weathermen.
- **Faulty parallelism**: "To be considered great, an NFL running back must be able to change direction, to run with power, a good IQ is helpful, see and hit the "holes," durability is important." Hint: Reread the sentence using just the subject and each phrase, one at a time. Here's the correct way to write it (and test parallelism): "An NFL running back must run with power, (...must) be able to change direction, (...must) be smart, (...must) be able to see and hit holes, and (...must) be durable."
- **Too many simple sentences begging to be combined**: "The two friends were practicing hockey. They were on an ice floe. It was near their village. It was huge. It was flat." Try a simple combination sentence instead: "The two friends practiced hockey on a huge, flat ice floe near their village."
- **Problems with the most confused or misused words**: its/it's; you're/your; weather/whether; their/they're/there; to/two/too; principal/principle; affect/effect; conscience/conscious; accept/except; than/then; who's/whose; among/between; eminent/imminent/immanent; all ready/already; lay/lie; all together/altogether.

- **Misspelled words**. Check every word. Ask yourself: "If I had to bet $100 that I spelled that word correctly, would I pull out my wallet?" No? Then you'd better look it up in the dictionary! Watch out for words your spell-check program may not catch, such as "too" instead of "to" or "your" instead of "you're."
- **Incorrect punctuation**. Review the rules regarding placement of commas, quotation marks, periods, and other punctuation. Make sure you follow those rules throughout your paper.

Should you include graphics?

If a picture is worth a thousand words, can you just include four pictures and forget having to write that 15-page paper? No, but nice try. However, there may well be instances when including a chart, graph, diagram, or some such element will both spruce up the look of your paper and help illuminate a concept better than words ever could.

Consider including some form of graphics:

- When describing a complex process, such as how water from a dam creates hydroelectric power.
- When a chart or graph can better encapsulate mathematical data, such as changes in respiration rates, in one-minute intervals, during a marathon.
- When a map would help the reader visualize what you're talking about, such as the changes in downtown New York since 9/11.
- Whenever it would make the paper look more presentable, help you organize your data, and/ or help the reader understand your point.

Your inclusion of a graphic element of any kind—chart, graph, diagram, table, drawing, photograph, etc.—should *accentuate* the text, not merely be an attempt to cover up bad writing and/or poor organization. If it's not explained, placed in the proper context, nor supported in the text itself, adding an illustration adds nothing.

Prepare the *almost*-final draft

Now get back on the computer and make all of those corrections you marked as you completed each of the previous steps. (Or retype your paper incorporating all of those corrections.) As you prepare this draft of your paper, incorporate the following three steps:

1. Format the paper according to your teacher's instructions—use the specified page length, margins, and line spacing. If you haven't been given any instructions in this area, follow these guidelines:
   - Type or print on one side of the paper only.
   - Use 8 1/2 x 11 paper.
   - Leave a one-inch margin all around—top, bottom, right, and left.
   - Indent the first word of each paragraph five spaces from the left margin.
   - Double-space all text. (Single-space footnotes, but double space between each.)
   - Number your pages in the upper right-hand corner of the paper, one half-inch from the top.

2. Incorporate your final footnotes, endnotes, or parenthetical notes. For specifics on how to do this, see Appendix A.

3. Give your paper a title, if you haven't already done so. Your title should be as short and sweet as possible, but should tell readers what they can expect to learn from your paper. Don't get cute or coy.

You may want to have a title and a subtitle—for example, "Women Air Force Service Pilots: The Almost-forgotten Veterans of World War II." If so, separate your subtitle from the title with a colon and two spaces.

Some teachers prefer that you put your title, name, date, and class number on a separate title page. Others want this information to appear at the top of the first page of your text. As always, ask your instructor which page format to follow. (And consult the style manuals listed in Appendix B for specific formats.)

Now, give yourself a big pat on the back! The toughest parts of your assignment are all behind you.

Make it perfect

To be a good proofreader, you need a sharp eye. Unfortunately, your poor eyes are probably pretty tired by now. And you've become so familiar with your paper that it may be difficult for you to see it clearly. You're likely to read phrase by phrase, rather than word by word (and certainly not letter by letter). And that means that you'll likely skip right over some typos and other errors.

Another problem is that our brain often convinces us we're seeing what we *expect* to see. I recently published a book that, according to the spine, was titled "The War World II 100." When it was handed to me and I was asked to read it aloud, looking right at it, I "read," "The World War II 100."

In this section, I'll show you some tricks that will help you overcome these problems and catch all those little bugaboos in your manuscript.

Read your paper aloud

Go to a quiet room and read your paper aloud. Not in your head—actually speak the words you have written. Sound them out, syllable by syllable. You'll quickly identify an uncomfortable number of typos and misspelled words.

Circle any errors that you find with a brightly colored pen or pencil. You want to be able to spot them easily and quickly when you type up your final draft.

Work backward

This is another great trick. Read your paper from back to front, starting with the last word on the last page, working backward toward your introduction. This will force you to focus on each individual word, rather than on the meaning of your phrases and sentences.

Use your computer's spell-check

If you're working on a computer that has a spell-check program, be sure to use it. But don't rely on it alone! Yes, the computer will pick up misspelled words. But what if you've used the wrong *word* altogether—used "their" when you meant "there"? If you've *spelled* it right, the computer won't pick up your error (though a grammar/usage program probably will).

Have someone else read your paper

Ask a parent, sibling, or other relative to read your paper. Or trade papers with a classmate—you'll look at his if you can show him yours. Someone who has never seen your paper before is much more likely to catch a mistake than someone who has read it again and again. Just be careful about the person you pick and the instructions you give her. You don't want to hear from your lovely but anal-retentive friend—an hour before your paper is due—how *she* would have organized it.

Prepare your perfect copy

After you've proofread your paper several times (*at least* three times), type or print out a clean draft. Then proofread it *again,* to make sure you caught every single error. Miss one or two? Print those pages again *and proofread again.* Continue until you're sure your paper is error-free. Then proofread it one more time (and I'm willing to bet real money you will still find at least one mistake).

Remember that you are checking three distinct areas: content, spelling and grammar, and format. Don't do a great job on the first two and forget to number your pages or include your bibliography!

Get it all together

Be sure to put your final draft on good quality, white bond. Don't use that erasable typing paper—it smudges easily.

If you've written your paper on a computer, avoid printing your final draft on a low-quality dot matrix or bubble-jet printer. Manuscripts printed on such printers are sometimes hard to read—and the last thing you want to do is make it difficult for your teacher to read your paper. (Some instructors do not even accept such copies.)

Last Minute Tip: If you're writing a paper on a weekend or overnight, your content is unlikely to earn you a top grade. You'd better concentrate on the presentation and hope it conceals some of your paper's basic shortcomings.

You can also save your paper on a floppy disk or Zip disk and take it to a quick-print shop. Providing you're working on a compatible computer system, they can print out your paper on a laser printer, which produces typeset-quality printing. If your school has a computer lab, there might be a few good-quality printers available there as well.

If you don't have access to a good printer, or if you're just a lousy typist, you may want to have your final draft prepared by a professional typist or computer service bureau. Just make sure the one you select can have your paper done in plenty of time to meet your final deadline!

As soon as you complete your final draft, head right for the copy shop. Pay the buck or two it costs to make a copy of your paper. In the event that you lose or damage your original manuscript, you will have a backup copy.

Here's a great tip: Type the file name for your report right at the top of your copy. That way, if you ever have to refer back to the report, you'll know exactly where to find it on your hard drive. This is especially important if you're not using long file names and have to remember what Jdtxthis.doc stands for!

Turn in your assignment

Put your paper in a new manuscript binder or folder, unless your instructor asks you to do otherwise. Then, turn in your paper—on time, of course!

Chapter 7

Last Minute Strategy

Now that you know what you *should* have done, what can you do now that you've procrastinated so long you don't have nearly enough time to do the job you *should* have?

Did I suggest you ask for an extension? Of course I did. Did you? No? As my Uncle Ray used to say, what are you, stupid? If there is any chance you can turn a last-minute paper into simply a *late* paper (without the teacher taking anything off your grade), what possible reason could you have not to take it? ASK. You never know. Your instructor may actually have gotten up on the right side of the bed for the first time in his life and be in the mood to make *you* the beneficiary of his largesse.

Speaking of your instructor, what kind of person is he? What are his favorite books? Authors? TV shows? Sports teams? Do you know *anything* about him? You certainly should—such knowledge might affect the topic you choose, the resources you quote, the way you structure the paper, how you write it, whether you use graphics, and many other details. Ask former students some of the above questions—will it hurt to actually do something that the teacher is prone to like? Hey, you need all the edge you can get!

In the next chapter, I'll help you confront tighter and tighter deadlines—less than two weeks, a week, a weekend, a single day and night—and show you *exactly* what you need to do (and *not* do) to still turn in a solid paper.

In this chapter, I want to discuss some *general* last-minute strategies and considerations pertinent to *any* paper for which you just haven't got the time. Remember: Because your paper *is* "last minute," you are undoubtedly going to be forced to compromise *somewhere*. The only questions are where, and how much?

Spend a little thinking time

The *less* time you have, the *more* important it is to allocate it wisely. In general, the amount of time you should spend thinking about, outlining and preparing your paper is inversely proportional to the time you have left. This may freak you out—if you have so little time left, how can you possibly devote a substantial portion of it to "planning"? I've got to get to the library! I've got to take notes! Darn it, I've got to write!

No, you've got to *plan*. Take the time to think about the choices you're making—from a topic to resources to the right words. Set realistic goals for the time you have to work with. To develop an organized, logical approach to your paper. To do things nearly right the first time through. To take a deep breath before you panic!

Here are some key tips to follow while you think about your paper:

- Find a place to work where you won't be interrupted—the library, a secluded corner of your parents' home, a friend's place. The last thing you need is trying to write a last-minute paper while the dorm is imploding!
- Unhook the phone. It's the greatest distraction in the world. And it's guaranteed to ring just as you've figured out the perfect way to organize

your paper. Hello? Oh, drat, what came after
that paragraph?

- Tell your friends you're incommunicado. Don't
  call, don't write, don't come over with pizza. Become a hermit for the day or days you need to
  concentrate.

- Write down your detailed schedule and monitor
  how well you're doing. Under the circumstances,
  you have little choice but to toe the line. Don't
  blow your schedule. It's the only one you've got!

- Take the breaks you need, eat when you need, rest
  when you can. If your body falls into catatonia,
  you'll never get the paper done! Take care of yourself under these extreme circumstances.

"Peaking" at the right time

Presuming you're "last minute" but not yet totally des-
perate (you have less than a week or two but more than a
weekend), one key to making the most of *whatever* time you
have left is knowing when you get your best work done and
acting on that knowledge. In other words, what are your "peak
productive times"?

When are you most likely to be effective, enthusiastic,
detail-oriented...awake? Try to schedule your key tasks during this time. Are you better in the morning? Get up even
earlier than usual and get that research done! An evening
person? Take a nap during the day and work all night if you
have to. Whatever you do, don't expect (or try) to do your best
work at your worst time.

What if you have so many other commitments—even as
you try to find the time to write this paper—that you simply
can't take advantage of your "prime time"? Well, use whatever time is available, and use it wisely. If your prime time is
already chock full of other classes, work, etc., your next best
option is to identify and utilize the time closest to your "prime

time." If nothing is available—you're a morning person but you're stuck doing this paper during a single evening—you don't *have* another option. Just do it!

Choosing a topic

The less time you have, the more important it is to choose a topic about which you already know *something*, preferably a great deal. Can you adapt a paper you did for another course this year? For another course *last* year? Can you somehow find a topic pertinent to the course that incorporates the knowledge you've gained from your hobbies or outside interests?

Doing research

Whatever you can do to reduce the necessary research time will help you. If you already know a great deal about a topic—whether you've ever written a paper about it—write a detailed outline of a potential paper. Then *just research the areas you don't know*. Because you will save so much time on research—which is where you're supposed to spend the *most* time—this strategy might actually allow you to write an A paper overnight, an accomplishment I would normally call a fantasy.

If your instructor has specified you have to use *primary* sources (people who were part of or witness to events) rather than *secondary* (those writing about the events after the fact), you're not necessarily in trouble unless the topic is so current you need to schedule interviews. They usually need to be set up much further in advance than a few days! However, you may be able to extract yourself from even this quagmire if you can e-mail your proposed interviewee(s) a short series of questions and ask (beg?) that they respond via e-mail. Alternatively, short phone interviews might be scheduled, even at the last minute.

Even though your time is limited and you're concentrating on this paper, you should try to prepare for the next time you find yourself in the same situation. (Oh, come now, you *know* you'll blow it at least once more before you see the light!) If you find an excellent library or online resource for that course (and a future paper) or even one of your other courses, jot down the pertinent information and throw it into a folder at home marked "Research resources." Any time you can save the *next* time—and finding pertinent resources is certainly a time-consuming part of writing any paper—will be invaluable.

Taking notes and writing your first draft

This suggestion is not for the weak at heart, but could be a significant timesaver for the good typists among you: Take notes right on a notebook computer. Paraphrase as you go, document as you go, write as you go. When you think you've got everything you need, print out all your notes, then cut and paste them on large sheets of paper. That way, you can move them around as you see fit, have some room to write transitions and spot gaps you need to fill. It's a fast and dirty way to do a rough draft that essentially eliminates writing notes at all. (Or eliminates the rough draft, depending on your point of view.)

An alternative for the slightly squeamish: Use the note-taking system I described earlier only to record your own thoughts and ideas. Pack your pockets with change when you go to the library. When you find pertinent information in a book, photocopy every passage that you would have normally taken notes on. When you've photocopied all the material from all the resources you located, head home and do the same cut and paste discussed above. This will at least put your paper in the proper order. Then start writing your rough draft, paraphrasing as you go.

This latter method does not save nearly as much time as the former, but is a reasonable alternative for those of you who a) don't have notebook computers or b) can write faster than you can type, so why bother? It also makes it far less likely that you will, in your sleep-deprived state, inadvertently plagiarize, since you'll have copies of the original writing right in front of you.

If you choose to use either of these methods, it's important to construct a reasonable outline before you get started so you have some idea of how to organize everything you've just typed or photocopied. On your computer, you can actually type the main topic letter before each note, then sort all the notes by general area, again saving you time as you cut and paste. You still will have to order the notes within each section, but the greater part of each section's notes should at least be in the proper piles. You can then do a full topic outline right from the paper you've just written to see if the organization you chose made sense and to identify any gaps you need to fill.

Given your lack of time, you don't really have enough of it to organize your paper in a complicated way, especially if you then have to start moving a lot of paragraphs around to fit the structure. Choose the simplest structure that will work with your topic, the one that is the most logical. Better to keep it simple and do it well than do a lousy job on a paper with a complicated structure.

Editing and revising

The less time you have, the fewer the number of drafts you should expect to produce. If you have a day and a night or even a weekend, you should plan to only produce a rough draft; a single, best-you-can-do-with-the-time-you've-got rewrite; and a solid final draft following a single detailed proofread. A good grammar and usage program (along with your spell check, of course) would really help you here.

Under those circumstances, better to spend as much time as you can allocate to researching and organizing the paper. Remember what I've said more than once in previous chapters: Your grade will usually depend far more on these two areas than on the actual writing.

When it's time to say enough

"Of every four words I write, I strike out three."
—Nicolas Boileau

Yes, and Flaubert filled a wastebasket with crumbled first drafts until he was satisfied with a single page of writing.

You can't afford that kind of behavior. There *are* no last-minute perfectionists. The less time you have, the more likely something is going to lag—you'll need to take fewer notes from fewer resources for fewer drafts of a paper that you will proof fewer times. Be ready to say enough—enough research, enough rewrites, enough checking. You simply have no choice.

The less time you have available, the more important it is to plan how much time you're going to spend on each area. While I'll give you suggestions for how to divide up your chores, you should create your own schedule, based on your own strengths and weaknesses, before you do anything. Then stick to it. If you gave yourself 10 hours to take notes (because you know you need extra time to type them into your computer), don't pass your deadline or you'll never get the paper finished!

When you can't go on

The tighter your schedule, the more likely you will hit the occasional roadblock—your eyes will start to close, your brain to wilt, your will to finish that paper to disappear. Here are some quick ways to regroup and reenergize:

- Take a nap. When you get too tired to do more than stare at your computer screen, it's time to take a break and get a little shut-eye. We're not talking hours here, but a 20-minute nap isn't going to kill your deadline. Go to bed!
- Have a drink. A little caffeine won't hurt you— a cup of coffee or tea, hot chocolate, even a soda. Just don't mainline it—after a few cups, it seems

to have the opposite effect. Ever try to nap with a caffeine buzz? It isn't pretty.

- Turn off/down the heat. Get a little air and revive your brain.
- Take a walk. Or lift some weights. Or do a few squat thrusts. Anything to get your adrenaline flowing a little.

When time is precious

Just because you're on a last-minute schedule doesn't mean other responsibilities will vanish from your calendar. You may still have work, other assignments, tests, and family responsibilities to consider. Which makes it essential that you use every minute you have, especially "in-between" time when you're waiting in line or for an appointment, commuting, or just not doing much of anything. Take those opportunities to:

- Make phone calls.
- Read something.
- Mail letters.
- Pick up groceries.
- Clean up.
- Review your schedule.
- Proofread.
- Think!
- Relax!

Chapter 8

When Deadlines
Get Tighter

If you had more than two weeks until your paper is due, you could follow one of the plans I showed you earlier. You would have sufficient time to devote to each step. And probably have the time to do a superior job (or a poor one if you choose). You wouldn't have to do anything extraordinary if you had that much time available.

But that *isn't* the case right now, is it? You're running out of time, and you need to employ some special strategies.

If you have two weeks (or a little less)

You shouldn't be in panic mode yet, unless, of course, the kind of paper you're talking about producing is a master's thesis or its equivalent. In which case, feel free to panic.

With two weeks left, there is still time to do an A+ paper without having to horribly cut corners. Here's a strategic plan:

Finalize topic, produce temporary thesis and outline	2 days
Do detailed library research	5 days

Prepare detailed outline (from note cards)	1 day
Write first draft	1 day
Do additional research (if necessary)	1/2 day
Write additional drafts	2 days
Spell-check, proofread "final" draft	1/2 day
Have someone *else* proofread	1/2 day
Produce a final draft, proofread, turn in	1/2 day
Extra time available	1 day

You should notice a few things about this schedule. The amount of time allocated to finalizing your topic is the same as it was when you had four weeks left. That's because choosing the right topic and preparing a coherent temporary thesis and outline takes on even more importance when you have less time.

You still have *some* time for additional research, but certainly not a lot. The emphasis at this point is clearly on getting it right the first time. You still have two days to work with your note cards and create a first draft, an additional two days for rewrites, plus almost two days for proofing. In other words, virtually the whole second week is writing, editing and proofing. This is doable, even if it's a 25-page paper. (Although a mere five days to research that long a paper is cutting it mighty close.)

When you only have a week

Now we're getting a little closer to Panicville. Here's a new schedule, and it sure doesn't leave a lot of time for pizza and a movie:

Finalize topic, produce temporary thesis and outline	1 day
Do detailed library research	2 days
Prepare detailed outline (from note cards)	1/2 day
Write first draft	1/2 day
Do additional research (if necessary)	No time!

Write additional drafts	2 days
All proofreading steps	1 day
Extra time available	None!

You are still devoting a significant amount of time—1/7 of the total amount allotted—to choosing a topic and organizing your preliminary research. We're clearly at the point where finding a topic about which you already know a great deal would be a huge benefit.

And research time is now at a premium. Remember my two suggestions from Chapter 7—taking notes directly on a laptop or using photocopying? This is about the time when you might have to resort to one or the other. With five full days to research and write all your drafts, anything that will help you combine steps or reduce the time necessary to complete them must be considered.

Have you considered pairing up with a study partner and doing two separate papers that consider opposite sides of the same question? While the papers themselves might have very little in common—since they're delineating opposite arguments—much of the work necessary to find appropriate resources and even to take notes (presuming the other is a decent note taker) can be shared. Since research is the greatest proportionate part of any paper, finding a way to reduce your research time without compromising the content of your paper would be an incredible boon!

Since you would now have the ability to brainstorm with another student who is (hopefully) at least as smart as you, this technique could save you time and effort as you develop a preliminary outline and help you sift through ideas and points of view. This idea may be especially attractive to someone else who has procrastinated as much as you and is under similar time pressure.

Do *not* develop virtually identical approaches to virtually identical topics, even if you are preparing them for different teachers. The possibility of being charged with plagiarism (let alone the possibility that a portion of your paper may *appear* to be plagiarized even if it's not) is just too great to justify the help. (It's pretty obvious why this would be even more dangerous if you're both preparing papers for the same teacher, isn't it?)

Where else can you realistically save time when you have barely a week? I wouldn't suggest cheating on the single day you've allocated for proofing—you may well do all of the steps more quickly, but I wouldn't skip any of them. If anything, I would be even more careful during this stage. Since it's doubtful you've been able to do the extensive research and well-crafted writing that earns an A+, you simply want to aim for a solid B, at worst. You can't afford losing points for spelling errors, etc., and winding up with a C (if you're lucky).

As I've stressed before, the *less* time you have to write, the *more* time you need to devote to structure, organization, and your first and last paragraphs. Grip them at the beginning and leave them with a solid, well-wrought ending. And if your teacher knows my hamburger metaphor and asks, "Where's the beef?" Well, you tried.

If you have a weekend left

Boy, you certainly do believe in cutting it close, don't you? This is when it becomes difficult to do much more than make sure you get a passing grade.

First and foremost, you have too little time to do even modest research for a college-level paper. Probably not enough time for most high school assignments, either. So it is paramount that you find a way to discuss something you already know a great deal about. Without such "pre-knowledge," you will be burning the candle at both ends and, undoubtedly, getting singed.

The topic should also be something you feel passionately about. When you have to write a great deal of text in a short period of time, it sure is easier to write about something that makes you angry, leaves you indignant, or stokes your competitive fires. If you can pick a thesis that strongly touches something in your heart, the battle may be half-won.

Is there a short list of resources *with which you're already familiar* that you can use as the basis for your paper? These should ideally be works you already possess, those that are in the restricted section of the library (so that you don't have to worry about one of your colleagues running off with it just when you need it) or at an online site you know like the back of your head, er, hand. You have little time to start creating a resource list from scratch.

Below, I'm going to give you a bare-boned, single-day battle plan. If you have a full weekend (or even three days), just adjust it accordingly.

If your paper is due tomorrow

First and foremost, you can't type your paper on any kind of typewriter. Nor can you use a typing service. You simply haven't the time. You absolutely must do your paper on a computer. If you don't have one of your own and aren't used to using one (and if that's the case, I'm presuming you're over 40), you are about to get one heck of an introduction to your word processing program!

My previous idea of taking notes directly onto a computer would certainly be a bonus plan now!

Remember what I said in Chapter 1 about the five fundamentals, including following your teacher's instructions to the letter? Well, you may have to break that rule here. If you are trying to write a 15- to 20-page paper overnight, it's probably impossible to do a really good job. You may want to consider doing a *great* job on a paper that is *shorter*. You have to know your teacher before you try this—if she's known for being an absolute stickler or has a history of giving out Fs for relatively insignificant errors, grind out the best 15-page paper you can under the circumstances. But if you think he is the type who would rather see a well-wrought 10-page paper than a stream-of-consciousness 20-pager, you might consider ignoring the suggested length and doing a better job on a shorter paper.

Here's an hour-by-hour schedule to write a paper in a single day (and only part of the night):

6:00 – 6:30 am	Shower, shave, eat breakfast, snarl, program your answering machine to screen all calls, stick a DO NOT DISTURB sign on your door.
6:30 – 8:00	Schedule your day. Determine the topic and angle of your paper—preferably a topic you know a lot about and/or one with which you have a strong emotional or intellectual connection. Line up trusted references.
8:00 – 10:00	Go through all resources at hand, take notes, compose detailed outline as you go.
10:00 – 12:00	If necessary, find additional resources at library or online. Take notes and finalize preliminary outline. Sort notes accordingly.
12:00 – 1:00	LUNCH. Relax and eat. Disengaging your mind for a little while is an important step if you plan to work for another dozen hours or so.
1:00 – 3:00	Write rough draft. And I *really* mean rough. This should entail little more than transferring your notes to the computer, with modest paraphrasing or rewriting as you go. Do not even consider worrying about the "right" words, grammar, spelling, or the like. Just get everything down on paper as fast as you can type.
3:00 – 4:00	Read through a printed copy of your rough draft. Move things around, do a little rewriting, look for research holes.

4:00 – 4:30	BREAK. But this time, while you drink (a little) and snack (a little), keep thinking about your paper and stay in the groove.
4:30 – 6:00	If you need to do additional research, do it now and incorporate your new notes directly into your rough draft. If you don't (or finish before the allocated time), print out a copy of your "final" rough draft and begin editing and rewriting.
6:00 – 8:00	Edit and rewrite.
8:00 – 9:00	DINNER (You don't usually treat yourself this well when you don't have a last-minute paper, do you?).
9:00 – 10:00	Detailed grammar and style check.
10:00 – 11:00	Work exclusively on rewriting, editing, and checking the first and last paragraphs.
11:01	Go to bed. Really. Yes, I know you haven't proofed. Trust me.
6:00	Rise and shine, last-minute warrior. Do all your morning ablutions, then proof your paper as many times as you can until the moment it's due (or you have to print it out and take care of other commitments). Try to ensure that at least one other person proofreads it for you.

Why did I suggest you go to bed at such a sensible time? If you actually started working at 6:30 that morning, you will have been going for nearly 17 hours by 11:00 pm. Even with three breaks scheduled throughout the day, you are going to be one tired hombre by the time you finish writing. Do you really think that's the best time to look for hard-to-spot spelling and grammatical errors? No, it isn't. But after a reasonable night's sleep, you'll be in a much better frame of mind (not to mention amazed that you actually wrote a paper in a single day!) and ready to tackle those last proofing steps.

Chapter 9

Let This Last Minute Paper Be Your Last!

You don't *really* want to ever go through this again, do you? I didn't think so. While I hope the ideas in this book have been helpful, I also fervently hope you don't make it a habit of needing them.

If this is not your *first* last-minute paper—and you've been known to pull frequent all-nighters to "prepare" for tests—your entire approach to studying could stand some serious improvement. Some people work well under pressure. Few people work well under *constant* pressure. And pushing yourself to the edge for paper after paper and test after test cannot rank highly on the pantheon of "Fun Things to Do...Every Weekend."

How did you get here?

Whether you're ready to admit it or not, you're doing *something* wrong if you've had to read this book! Are you frustrated at the end of nearly every day? Has your to-do list grown to the size of the telephone book? Do you even *have* a to-do list?

One or more of the following items is to blame for this sorry state of affairs:

- **No clear goals.** You must have a sense of purpose to accomplish anything. If you don't know where you're going, any road will take you there. But how will you know when you've arrived?

- **Lack of priorities**. If you aren't sure what a to-do list is, I think we've found the problem. But even the most detailed to-do list is of little value if it isn't prioritized—forcing you to do the most important things first, rather than the easiest.

- **No daily plan**. Beginning each day without a plan is a formula for frustration, a way to ensure that you may accomplish something, but probably not what you really *needed* to accomplish.

- **Perfectionism**. If you keep working on each assignment until it's "perfect," you'll soon find you can't ever stay on schedule. There is always a better word to write, another page to study, another note to take, another book to read. That doesn't mean you should spend three times as much time as everyone else on every assignment...just to get the same grade.

- **Disorganization**. Even if you've established a relatively effective time-management system, complete with prioritized to-do lists and calendars, if you can never *find* your lists or calendar, you are going to fall behind.

- **Interruptions**. If your best-laid plans can be instantly derailed by a phone call or unexpected invitation, you'll never manage to stick to a schedule, no matter how simple. Learn how to eliminate many interruptions and control those you can't.

- **Procrastination**. You don't need to become a robo-student, rolling emotionlessly from class to library to study hall. But if you do find yourself re-reading this book monthly—because you have yet another last-minute paper to write—you may want to deal with your tendency to put things off!

If you deal with everything or almost everything at the last minute, your grades will surely reflect your poor focus and planning. So before you close this book forever, please consider adopting the following ideas to change your last-minute habit into one of preparedness:

- Learn or create a **simple time-management system** that you will actually use and follow. I don't really care whether it's "mine" (see the fifth edition of my book *How to Study* for a simple system you can implement immediately). Just find something that works for you and use it. The busier you are—and the more often you find yourself crunching deadlines—the more important this is.

- **Write everything down**, preferably in one place. Whether you take my above advice, at least do this—it's the simplest way to avoid forgetting important dates and assignments.

- Make **goal-setting** a natural part of your life. And not just those far-away, ephemeral fantasies that are easy to establish *because* they "exist" so far in the future. Get into the habit of setting daily and weekly goals.

- Figure out how to **manage priorities**. Clearly, you're doing something wrong if you are consistently facing deadlines with no time to spare. Make some sort of prioritizing a key part of your time management system. You can't always do what you want, but at least you'll do what you need (with apologies to Mick J.).

- Tackle your **toughest assignments first**. If you do so on a consistent basis, you will have fewer problems as deadlines loom. After all, the deadlines will be for the easiest projects or quizzes, not some original 25-pager or a midterm!

- Figure out how to **manage distractions**. As a time management guru once put it, "Don't respond to the urgent and forget the important." Even if you're doing a relatively good job of managing your time and setting priorities, it's easy for a phone call, TV show, or social event to completely destroy your determination to "buckle down and get that paper done tonight." Either learn how to avoid or deal with them, or how to rearrange your schedule when you give in to them.

- Identify your **"peak" times** and study accordingly. Don't even think of pulling an all-nighter if you're normally in bed by 10. You won't make it.

- No matter how late you are, **you always have time to plan**. And the sooner you make time to plan, the easier it will be to avoid being late!

- Learn how to use whatever time you have **more effectively**. If it takes most others a week to craft a short, well-written paper, why is it taking you a month? When you reach a lull in your schedule, plan to learn (or relearn) some basic study skills. Their lack may be a key part of your last-minute problems!

- Create **your own reference library** and a list of helpful Web sites. They'll come in handy for homework, projects, papers, and test review.

- **Be (or become) a reader**. You'll have more access to information, ideas, criticism, philosophies and analyses, all of which will help you in every aspect of your schoolwork, but especially writing papers.

- Consider creating and consistently expanding **your own shorthand** for taking notes. This will come in remarkably handy both in class, when working from textbooks, or when preparing a paper or report.

This is a very short list of items that will make a significant difference, not just in your study habits, but in your life. I hope you learn them. I hope you use them.

And I certainly hope you'll never need to do *anything* last minute again!

Appendix A

Document Your Resources

You must give credit to the source of any fact, expression, or idea you use in your paper that is not your own, even if you do not quote it directly.

For many years, the preferred way to credit sources was the *footnote.* Two other forms of documentation, *endnotes* and *parenthetical notes*, are popular now as well. For convenience, I'll refer to all three of these forms collectively as "source notes."

Whose rules are they, anyway?

Different authorities have set out different rules for bibliography listings. The same is true for source notes. Many subject areas have their own manuals you will be expected to follow. Here's a short list, by subject, of key style manuals:

- *Biology:* Huth, Edward J. <u>Scientific Style and Format: The CBE Manual for Authors, Editors and Publishers, 6th Ed.</u> New York: Cambridge Univ. Press, 1994

- *Chemistry:* Dodd, Janice S., ed. <u>The ACS Style Guide: A Manual for Authors and Editors, 2nd Edition.</u> Washington, DC: American Chemical Society, 1998.

- *Engineering:* How to Write and Publish Engineering Papers and Reports, 3ʳᵈ Ed. Phoenix: Oryx Press, 1990
- *Law:* Harvard Law Review Staff. Uniform System of Citation: The Bluebook, 16ᵗʰ Ed. Cambridge: Harvard Law Review, 1996.
- *Mathematics:* American Mathematical Society. A Manual for Authors of Mathematical Papers, 8ᵗʰ Ed. Providence: American Mathematical Society, 1980.
- *Medicine:* Iverson, Cheryl, et al. American Medical Association Manual of Style: A Guide for Authors and Editors, 9ᵗʰ Ed. Lippincott, Williams and Wilkins, 1997.
- *Music:* Holoman, D. Kern, photographer. Writing About Music: A Style Sheet from the Editors of 19ᵗʰ Century Music. Berkeley: Univ. of California Press, 1988
- *Physics:* American Institute of Physics. AIP Style Manual, 4ᵗʰ Ed. New York: Springer Verlag, 1990.
- *Political Science:* Michael K. Lane. Style Manual for Political Science. American Political Science Association, 1993.
- *Psychology:* American Psychological Association. Publication Manual of the American Psychological Association, 5ᵗʰ Ed. Washington, DC.: American Psychological Association, 2001. (The APA style is the second most used, after the MLA. Many schools and some colleges require its use for all papers.)

The one you will tend to use for all humanities courses—and that you may well be able to use for virtually all courses—is the *MLA Handbook*. Or, as it's properly known, *MLA Handbook for Writers of Research Papers, 5ᵗʰ Edition* (by Joseph Gibaldi, Modern Language Association, 1999).

There are a plethora of other major style manuals, like the *Chicago Manual of Style* (which I use) and those put out by the New York Times, Associated Press, and many other news organizations.

Ask your instructor whose rules you are to follow.

If your teacher doesn't have a preference, use the manual whose rules seem easiest to use. But follow the same rules consistently throughout your paper—don't use a footnote on one page and an endnote on another.

I'm going to give you the Modern Language Association of America (MLA) rules for three basic types of materials: a book, a magazine article, and a newspaper article. You can consult the *MLA Handbook* or other reference books for specific examples of how to prepare notes for more complicated types of material.

A reminder of what needs documentation

You need a source note when you put any of the following in your paper:

- Quotations taken from a published source.
- Someone else's theories or ideas.
- Someone else's sentences, phrases, or special expressions.
- Facts, figures, and research data compiled by someone else.
- Graphs, pictures, and charts designed by someone else.

There are some exceptions: You don't need to document the source of a fact, theory, or expression that is common knowledge. And you don't need a source note when you use a phrase or expression for which there is no known author.

For example, if you mention that Paris is the capital of France, Anne Frank died during the Holocaust or Abraham

Lincoln was the 16th U.S. President, you don't need to document the sources of that information. Ditto for time-worn phrases such as, "When in Rome, do as the Romans do" or a well-known quote such as, "We have nothing to fear but fear itself."

For a test of whether a statement needs a source note, ask yourself whether readers would otherwise think that *you* had come up with the information or idea by yourself. If the answer is "yes" (and you didn't), you need a source note. If you're in doubt, include a source note anyway.

Footnotes

A footnote is a source note that appears at the "foot" (bottom) of a page of text. The footnote system works like this: You put a raised (superscript) number at the end of the statement or fact you need to document. This serves as a "flag" to readers—it tells them to look at the bottom of the page for an explanation of the source of the data.

In front of that footnote, you put the same superscript number you assigned to the statement or fact in your text. This tells the reader which footnote applies to which statement or fact.

There is no limit to the number of footnotes you may have in your paper. Number each footnote consecutively, starting with the number 1. For every footnote "flag" in your paper, be sure there is a corresponding source note at the bottom of the page.

What goes into a footnote

The same information contained in a source's bibliographic listing is included in a footnote, with two differences: the author's name is shown in normal order (first name first, followed by middle name or initial and last name), and the exact page number on which the information appeared is cited.

Most of the information for your footnotes will come from your bibliography cards, but you'll have to look at your note cards to get the actual page numbers from which various facts came. Arrange these elements as follows:

1. Name of the author(s), first name first.
2. Title of the book or article.
3. Publication information—place of publication, name of the publisher, date of publication, and so on.
4. The number of the page(s) on which the information appeared in the work.

Typing your footnotes

The following general rules apply to all footnotes:

- Put footnotes four lines below the last line of text on the page.
- Indent the first line of a footnote five spaces.
- Single-space lines within an individual footnote; double-space between footnotes.
- Always put the superscript (raised) number of the footnote after the punctuation in your text.
- Abbreviate all months except May, June, July.

Punctuation guidelines for footnotes

There are specific rules of punctuation and style to follow when you write your footnotes.

For a book:

1. Number of the note (superscript).
2. Author's first name, middle name or initial (if any), last name (comma).
3. Title of the book (underlined); no period after the title.
4. In parentheses—place of publication (colon); name of the publisher (comma); year of publication.
5. Exact page(s) on which the information you're documenting appears (period). Do not write "page" or "pg." or "p."—just the number.

For a magazine article:
1. Number of the note (superscript).
2. Author's first name, middle name or initial (if any), last name (comma).
3. In quotation marks—title of the article (comma).
4. Name of the periodical in which the article appeared (underlined).
5. Day the periodical was published (for a weekly or biweekly periodical); month; year (colon).
6. Exact page number(s) from which the information was taken (period).

For a newspaper article:
1. Number of the note (superscript).
2. Author's first name, middle name or initial (if any), last name (comma).
3. In quotation marks—title of the article (comma).
4. Name of the newspaper in which the article appeared (underlined).
5. Name of the city and town in which the paper is published (if not part of the name of the paper and/or if the paper is not widely known)—enclose in brackets and do *not* underline.
6. Day the paper was published; month; year (comma).
7. Edition (abbreviate as "ed.") if more than one is published per day (colon).
8. Section and exact page from which the information was taken (period).

If there is other information on your card (the name of an editor or series), you need to include it in your footnote. Arrange information in the same order you would for a bibliography listing. (See Appendix B for the order.)

Second references

The second time you cite a particular reference as a source of information, use an abbreviated form of the footnote—just the author's last name and the page number on which the information appeared.

If you have taken information from two different books written by the same author, include the title of the specific book as well.

If there is no author provided for a work, cite the title and page number.

Endnotes

Within the body of your paper, you indicate the existence of an endnote in the same manner as for a footnote—with a superscript (raised) number. The only difference is that you put all of your source listings on a separate page at the end of the text, not at the bottom of each page.

Title the last page of your paper "Notes" and center it at the top of the page. Leave a one-inch margin on all sides of the paper (top, bottom, left, and right). List endnotes consecutively (note 1, then note 2, and so forth.). As with your footnotes, indent the first line of each note. Double-space the entire page (both within individual notes and between notes). Follow the same punctuation rules as those given for footnotes.

Parenthetical notes

Using parenthetical notes is probably the easiest way to document sources and the one now favored by the MLA, whose rules will probably govern any paper you write in the humanities (English, Literature, Political Science, etc.). In this system, you put a brief source note right in the body of your text, enclosed in parentheses (hence, the name—parenthetical note).

Generally, your reference includes only the last name of the author and the page number from which the information was taken. For example:

Two-thirds of all working-age disabled people are still unemployed. This is the same portion that was jobless when the law was passed (Smolowe 55).

To find complete details about the source, readers would look at your bibliography. In this case, they would look for a book or article by "(Somebody) Smolowe."

Make sure your note includes enough information so your readers will know exactly which source in your bibliography you are citing. For example, if your bibliography lists two different works, both written by authors with the last name of Smolowe, you should include the author's first name in your parenthetical note, (Jill Smolowe 55).

If you have two books, articles, whatever written by the same author, include the title of the book you are citing. You can use a one-, two-, or three-word abbreviation of the title, if you want. In this case, you might say (Smolowe, Noble Aims 55).

Your last minute preference

If you possibly can, use parenthetical notes. As you type your rough draft, follow any word or phrase you believe will eventually need a source note with the number of the appropriate bibliography card and the page number. For example:

According to General Sarnot, women pilots did not displace men at all. (3,422). Rather, they did the jobs no men wanted to do, and did them far better than anyone expected (6,25).

Now, when you are ready to finalize your paper, use your word processor's "find and replace" function to substitute the author's last name for each numbered card (and the comma, which must be omitted in your final paper). If your source lacks an author, use a shortened version of the book's title (underlined) or the name of an article or pamphlet (in quotes). If your source is a one-page article, you don't have to give any page number in your note.

If you are using footnotes or endnotes: When you come to the first "preliminary" note in your text, replace the letter and number code with the superscript numeral "1." Find the bibliography card with the same source number as that in your preliminary note. Type your footnote or endnote, using the data from the bibliography card. Use the same page number that you show in your preliminary note. Move on to the next note and number it "2", and so on.

Be especially careful about teachers who are anal-retentive about style manuals. It would be truly sorrowful if you managed to crank out a pretty good paper (overnight!) but got marked down because you consistently misplaced commas in your footnotes. You may rant and rave about the injustice of it all, and I may even be sympathetic, but I suspect neither one of us will get your grade improved.

Appendix B

Construct Your Bibliography

Your teacher may ask for a *"works consulted"* bibliography, a list of all reference materials you reviewed during your research, *even if nothing from them was incorporated in your paper.* Or, you may be asked to do a *"works cited"* bibliography, listing only the materials you mentioned in the footnotes, endnotes, or parenthetical notes.

If your teacher does not specify which type of bibliography to include, choose the first. It will be a better indication of the range of research you've done.

There are some very specific technical rules you must follow when preparing your bibliography. These rules are the same whether you are doing a "works consulted" or "works cited" bibliography.

Your bibliography listings contain virtually the same information as footnotes or endnotes, with two differences: 1) The format and punctuation are different, and 2) the page number references are different.

Somewhere along the line, people made up these rules. I'm sure there were good reasons for the things they decided, but the reasons aren't important. What *is* important is that you follow the rules—like them or not.

Remember, different authorities prefer different rules, so check with your teacher or professor to find out which rules he prefers. What follows are the rules according to the Modern Language Association (MLA).

Laying out your bibliography page

Your bibliography should be at the end of your paper, on a separate page or pages:

- One inch from the top of the page: Center the title "Works Cited" or "Works Consulted," depending upon which type of bibliography you're doing.
- Use the same margins as you did for the rest of your paper—probably one inch all the way around.
- Treat your bibliography pages as if they are a continuation of the text of your paper and number them accordingly—*don't* start repaginating.
- List sources alphabetically, by the author's last name. If no author is given, list by the first word in the title of the work (unless the first word is "A," "An," or "The," in which case list by the second word of the title).
- The first line of each listing should be flush with the left margin. Indent all other lines five spaces from the left margin.
- Double-space all listings and double-space between entries.
- Abbreviate all months except May, June, and July.

MLA style guidelines

You will take all of the information for your bibliography directly from your bibliography cards. Before typing, put your bibliography cards in the correct alphabetical order.

Then, just transfer all the information, card by card, following the style guidelines which I have listed here.

For a book:

1. Author's last name (comma), first name, and middle name or initial (period and skip a space).
2. Title of book, underlined (period, skip a space).
3. Place of publication (colon and skip a space); name of publisher (comma and skip a space); year of publication (period).

For a magazine article:

1. Author's last name (comma), first name, and middle name or initial (period and skip a space).
2. Title of article (in quotation marks, with a period before the ending quotation marks, then skip two spaces). Note: If name of the article ends with its own punctuation, such as a question mark, don't put in the period.
3. Title of periodical in which article appeared (underlined).
4. Day of publication (if one is given); month; year; (colon and space).
5. Page numbers on which article appeared (period). If article didn't appear on consecutive pages, just type the number of the first page followed by a plus (+) sign—for example, 23+.

You do not need to include the volume number of a magazine, unless it is a scholarly journal. But if in doubt, include it—better to have too much information than too little.

For a newspaper article:

1. Author's last name (comma), first name and middle name or initial (period and skip a space).
2. Title of article (in quotation marks, with a period before the ending quotation marks, then skip a

space). Note: If the article title ends with its own punctuation, such as a question mark, don't put in the period.

3. Title of newspaper in which article appeared, underlined.
4. Day of publication; month; year.
5. *If the paper publishes more than one daily edition:* Put a comma after the year, then type edition information (colon and space), then page numbers on which the article appeared. Include section letter or number if applicable—for example, A8.
6. *If the paper publishes only one daily edition:* Type a *colon* after the year (space), then section and page numbers on which article appeared.

If the newspaper isn't a nationally published or well-known paper, add the name of the city and state where it is published after the title. Enclose this information in brackets, but don't underline it. Example: Lawrence Times [Lawrence, NJ]. You do not need to include the volume or issue numbers of the newspaper.

I've prepared examples (below) of bibliography listings for resources you're most likely to use. Consult the most recent (fifth) edition of the *MLA Handbook* for a full discussion of the rules that apply to each of these entries.

Sample bibliography listings

Anthology selection

Brooks, Anne. "How to do a Crossword Puzzle." The Greatest How-tos of all Time. Ed. Karen Wolf. New York: Godfather Books, 1967.

Book with one author

Simplex, Vernon C. Wallace Stevens: A Life. New York: Jodi Books, 1999.

Book with two or three authors

Simplex, Vernon C. and Eugene Rutigliano. The Times of our Lives. New York: Harvest Publishers, 2002.

Book with four or more authors

Rutigliano, Eugene, et al. The Future of Mathematics. Boston: ASM Press, 2001.

Book with author and editor

James Joyce. The Complete Stories. Ed. Michael Lewis. New York: Laurie Publishing, 1999.

Book with editor(s) only

DeFelice, Nicole, ed. Modern Polish Poetry. New York: O'Sullivan Productions, 2001.

CD-rom

Wilder, Thornton. "Our Town". Great 20th Century Plays on CD-ROM. Los Angeles: Renaissance, 1995.

Computer database

Ryan, Thomas. "Softball Statistical Analysis." Statistical Abstracts 1999. Ryan Database, item 44-498.

E-mail

Olesky, Steven. Book Marketing Update. E-mail to the author. 24 Feb 2002

Encyclopedia

"Wilder, Thornton." The World Book Encyclopedia. 1994 ed.

Essay

LaRocca, Karen. "A New Perspective on Gilgamesh." The Art of the Literary. Ed. Carol Kennedy. Minneapolis: Certain Press, 1988.

Interview

Selver, Ellen. Personal interview. 14 June 2001

Lecture/speech

Harris, Caitlin. "The Future is Now." American Association of Travel Writers Convention. Atlanta, Georgia: 14 January 2001

Magazine article

Rutigliano, Tony. "It Don't Get Any Better." Pizza Today 24 Apr 1998: 22-28.

Newspaper article

Kennedy, Melissa. "High Fashion at the Crossroads." New York Newsday 14 May 1999, late ed.: B4.

Pamphlet

Dietary Tips for Daughters. Franklin Lakes, NJ: Lindsay Press, 1989.

Poem

Poe, Edgar Allen. "Annabel Lee." The Collected Works of Edgar Allen Poe. Ed. William C. Farnsworth. New York: Columbia, 1972. 218-221.

Play

Wilder, Thornton. Our Town. Great 20th Century Playwrights. Ed. Steven Turcotte. 8th ed. Austin: Kathleen Press, 1995.

Radio/Television program

"Remaking The Thin Red Line." Ramblings with Dave Field. ABC. WZRX, Boston. 22 Jan 1994.

Short story

Poe, Edgar Allen. "Hop Frog." The Collected Works of Edgar Allen Poe. Ed. William C. Farnsworth. New York: Columbia , 1972. 422-455.

Translation

Mann, Thomas. Collected Works. Ed. Jim Bert. Trans. Jenna LaRocco. New York: Thomas, 1969.

Citing online information

Because students are increasingly using online sources, every style guide for research papers has integrated electronic citations into their latest editions. Two other good sources to consult include Electronic Styles: A Handbook for Citing Electronic Information, 2nd Edition by Xia Li and Nancy Crane (Information Today Inc., 1996) and The Columbia Guide to Online Style by Janice Walker and Todd W. Taylor (Columbia University Press, 1998)

Here is a sample online citation:

Furfaro, John P. and Maury B. Josephson. "Reasonable Accommodation to Disability Act." New York Law Journal. http://homepages.go.com/~atlanticcity/040299c4.htm (2 April 1999)

Did you get them all?

Check your bibliography against the text of your paper. Be sure that you have included all the works cited in your source notes and followed all the rules when you entered them.

Index

C

D

E

F

W